SPIES, INVADERS AND SABOTEURS

SPIES, INVADERS AND SABOTEURS
The East of England during the First World War

BEN GRISTWOOD

Greenwich Exchange
London

Greenwich Exchange, London

First published in Great Britain in 2024
All rights reserved

Spies, Invaders and Saboteurs
© Ben Gristwood, 2024

This book is sold subject to the conditions that it shall not, by way of trade or otherwise, be lent, resold, hired out or otherwise circulated without the publisher's prior consent in any form of binding or cover other than that in which it is published and without a similar condition including this condition being imposed on the subsequent purchaser.

Printed and bound by imprintdigital.com
Cover design by December Publications
Tel: 07951511275

Greenwich Exchange Website: www.greenex.co.uk

Cataloguing in Publication Data is available
from the British Library

ISBN: 978-1-910996-64-5

for all those who have inspired my love of history and to all those who have helped and supported me along the way

CONTENTS

Introduction *11*

1 From Caesar to Napoleon *13*

2 The Coming of the Hun *21*

3 The Invasion of Eastern England *38*

4 Enemies on Our Doorstep? *58*

5 Paranoia and Hysteria *74*

6 Spy Fever *102*

7 Paranoia versus Reality *112*

Conclusion *129*

Bibliography *133*

INTRODUCTION

THIS BOOK DEVELOPS AND EXPANDS MY original work on the home front in the east of England throughout the First World War. I have added new resources as well as developing information and conclusions which I could, at the time of my dissertation, regrettably not include.

Spies, Invaders & Saboteurs, is a brief history of governmental and public responses to the fear of German invasion and espionage in the eastern English counties of Cambridgeshire, Bedfordshire, Hertfordshire and the coastal ones of Norfolk, Suffolk, and Essex, both in the years before and after the outbreak of hostilities. This book gives an overview of:

* The history of invasions of the British Isles and how this background embedded fears of invasion and espionage in the national psyche, and especially people living in the east of England

* Government concerns about, and responses to, possible invasion and espionage in the years leading up the Great War
* The government's response to fears of invasion and its counter-invasion preparations following the outbreak of war in August 1914
* How government fears and responses developed and changed during the war
* The effect governmental and military preparations had on the people living in the east of England during the war
* The reaction of the public in the east of England to fears of invasion and espionage during the Great War
* The spread of 'Spy Fever' both before and during the War
* The rationality of government, military and public fears in eastern England of German invasion and espionage in the context of what was known then, and what we know now

At the governmental level, I have referred to a range of documents, such as minutes of the Committee of Imperial Defence, Hansard parliamentary records as well as documents detailing government instructions distributed to the public.

In relation to espionage, I consulted papers from the Committee of Imperial Defence, sub-committees on espionage and public posters, as well as counter-espionage legislation and primary accounts of people in the Secret Services.

For public reactions, I have used local newspaper reports as well as other eyewitness accounts.

Popular literature on invasion and espionage is also reviewed as well as other primary accounts from the east of England.

Ben Gristwood
April 2024

1

FROM CAESAR TO NAPOLEON

The Background to 20th-century Invasion Fears within the United Kingdom and the East of England

WHILST THE MAIN FOCUS OF THIS book is about the effect of a possible German invasion as well as the fears of German espionage in the east of England during the First World War, it is important understand the origins of these fears. There are two main origins: the late nineteenth century rise of the unified, imperial Germany as the principal power in mainland Europe. The other is the compelling background of historical accounts of invasions, wars and accompanying treachery and resistance as well as the myths that surround these narratives.

Take a quick glance at the history of the British Isles – which goes back fairly reliably for two millennia. The history of Britain and its surrounding myths are moulded to a large extent by invasions endured, and invasions feared. Invasions and the stories told about them have helped to shape the way British national identity has developed. It has even become customary to divide British history into individual eras which have been ushered in by invasions. Britain has been invaded, or witnessed invasion attempts by other powers, on many occasions. The main events are sketched below.

Rome Invades
The first of these invasions that changed the history of Britain, that we conclusively know about are the Roman invasions of Britain, first attempted by Julius Caesar in 55 and 54 BCE as part of the Gallic wars. These initial invasions did not lead to a direct Roman governance of Britain, rather establishing client kings who would not aid the Celts on the continent in their wars against the invading Romans. The Roman Empire did not succeed in fully annexing the territories of the modern-day England and Wales until 43 CE nearly a century later, when Emperor Claudius' legions managed finally to occupy significant chunks of southern Britain. From then on, Rome gradually began to expand into Britain until it controlled all the area south of modern-day Scotland. Roman occupied Britain has remains of buildings and artefacts that bespeak an advanced civilisation. The territory dominated by Rome was won against severe resistance which led to the destruction of native cultures.

Collapse of the western Roman Empire
In the fifth century CE, the Western Roman Empire began to collapse. Consequently, the Roman legions which had occupied Britain for the last four centuries were ordered back to Rome. Their departure left behind land ripe for invasion and conquest. As Roman Britain weakened, the British soon found themselves under attack by the Celtic Picts of modern-

day Scotland and, seeking help, the British rulers hired Germanic mercenaries to fight off these northern invaders. However, after largely containing the Pictish threat, the Germanic tribes, realising their newfound power, soon settled in Britain. Over the next few centuries Britain was overrun with an invasion of migrating Germanic tribes, most notably the Angles, Saxons and Jutes, who after years of conquest formed many kingdoms across modern-day England which would come to be known as Anglo-Saxon England.

Arrival of the Vikings

As the newly victorious Anglo-Saxons began to stabilise their kingdoms and become assimilated into the British people, the invaders soon became the defenders. In the closing decade of the eighth century a new threat arrived from the north that would plague Britain for the next two centuries. In 793 AD Viking raiders from Scandinavia, called northmen, or simply heathens, by the Anglo-Saxons, raided the isolated monastery of Lindisfarne in the northern kingdom of Northumbria, shocking the Anglo-Saxon world and starting a chain of raids and small invasions which would occur throughout the ninth century. After nearly a century of devastating Viking raids across Britain, in 866 the Scandinavian kingdoms formed an enormous invasion force, ominously dubbed the Great Heathen Army by the Anglo-Saxons, which after only one year had overrun most of England.

Fightback by the Anglo-Saxons

By 878, however, the Anglo-Saxons had regained much of their lost strength and led by the near-legendary Wessex King,

Alfred the Great, they went on to defeat the Vikings at the battle of Eddington. The battle resulted in the adoption of the Dane Law which split England in half, with the north and eastern half being controlled by the Vikings, and the south and western portion being ruled by the Anglo-Saxons. From this point on England would always be half dominated, and, in some cases such as under the Danish king Cnut, fully controlled, by the Vikings, until 1003 when Edward the Confessor brought (by this point the now unified) Kingdom of England fully under the control of the Anglo-Saxons once more.

Norman Conquest
The final historical era-defining invasion came not long after this, when in 1066 William, Duke of Normandy - William the Conqueror, a claimant to the English throne, landed with troops along the south coast of England where he defeated the last Anglo-Saxon king, Harold Godwinson, at the Battle of Hastings. He went on to conquer the entirety of England. The Norman invasion displaced the Anglo-Saxon hierarchy replacing it with Norman aristocrats. The invaders committed what amounts to near genocide in the north of England. The English Church was changed also. The English kingdom would never be the same again. The year 1066 is a cited by many as perhaps the most important year in English history.

A Troubled Peace
Following the Norman Conquest, England was never again to be unwillingly subjugated by an invading force. However, it would frequently find itself at the threat of invasion. One

of these threats came from the kingdom of Scotland with whom England had incredibly poor relations with for most of the Middle Ages.

Scotland

In the late 13th and early 14th centuries Edward I of England, after his successful conquest of Wales, had attempted on multiple occasions to subjugate Scotland into his kingdom, provoking the wars of Scottish independence. The outcome of these wars resulted in centuries of attempted invasions between the two nations. England was subsequently invaded multiple times by Scotland and her allies, for instance: the Great Raid of 1322 by King Robert the Bruce, the Weardale campaign of 1327, the Neville's Cross campaign of 1346, the Franco-Scottish invasion of 1385, and finally the Flodden campaign of 1513, all of which proved to be unsuccessful.

France

Another age-old enemy which threatened to invade England multiple times was the Kingdom of France. There are three main periods of French threat. The first of these came amidst the chaos of the First Barons-War from 1215-1217. The English Barons, who were in open revolt against King John, supported an invasion of England by the French King Louis VIII, who after some initial victories ultimately proved unsuccessful in claiming the English throne.

The second and longest lasting of these threats from France stemmed from the Hundred Years War fought between England and France in the 13th and 15th centuries. Throughout this period and the following centuries, the constant conflict between England and France would result in many invasions being attempted on England, namely the French invasions of the English-held Channel Islands, the invasion threat of 1386 and the unsuccessful French invasion of 1405.

The third and most notorious of the French threats of invasion occurred in the modern era during the Napoleonic Wars, where between 1803 and 1805 enormous French forces under Napoleon Bonaparte prepared to invade the southern coast of England.

Rumours of invasion were felt across Great Britain. However, they never came to fruition. Whilst there are many other nations who have raided or attempted to invade England since the Norman Conquest, such as the Holy Roman Empire or the Dutch Republic. The most significant of these attempted invaders was Spain.

Spain: The Armada
In perhaps what is the most famous invasion attempt upon England, the Spanish Empire under Phillip II amassed an enormous fleet of galleons – the Armada - to land an invasion force from Flanders. The aim was to invade England to overthrow the Protestant monarch Elizabeth I and to restore England to the Catholic Faith. The invasion was unsuccessful due to disastrous weather, the poor leadership of Armada and the skill of the English Navy which provided a devastating blow to the Spanish. Victory against the odds is the mythic output of this conflict.

William of Orange
Finally, in 1688, the Dutch stadtholder, William of Orange, following a request from dissatisfied British nobles and

parliamentarians fearful of the Catholic King James II, landed in England forcing King James to flee to France. This is not quite the same as a bloody invasion of Britain, but it did establish William and his wife Mary as joint rulers of Great Britain. The effect In Ireland however was the opposite: political and armed conflict took place – which is still commemorated there. Alongside these invasion scares there have always been fears of spies and fifth columnists who would aid in these invasions.

Effects of Invasions

There is no doubt that these invasions, both the successful and the unsuccessful, as well as the almost constant invasion scares, has played a significant role in shaping the ethos and narratives which are quintessentially British.

On the positive side, Roman invasions of Britain, for example, for the first time brought a unified culture to Britain and for the first time brought large amounts of the island under the control of one authority. Subsequently, Anglo-Saxon and Viking invasions led for the first time to the creation of England as one unified kingdom as well as the beginnings of the English language. Finally, the Norman Conquest established the dynasties that would rule England and the rest of the British Isles to this day.

The subsequent threat of invasions following the Norman Conquest, such as the Napoleonic threats, shaped our military and foreign policies, with the Royal Navy becoming the predominant means to defend the country rather than a large standing army which was common in mainland Europe. These conflicts and fear of conflict have also contributed to the national identities of England, Scotland, and Wales.

Many of our national heroes being those who defended from foreign invasions. Boudicca, the legendary Celtic leader, is remembered in for her rebellion against the Romans. The legendary King Arthur was a Briton who supposedly fought against the Germanic invasions following the collapse of Roman Britain. Alfred the Great is best remembered for his defeat of the Viking forces in southern England. Scottish and Welsh national identities were also strongly forged in turn by English invasions and many of their national heroes such as the Scottish William Wallace and Robert Bruce or the Welsh Owain Glyndwr are remembered for their resistance to invading English armies.

Admittedly, this is necessarily a very simplified overview of British invasion history – but that is what is, overall, handed down the generations. Despite what we in the modern day might see as hysterical and nationalistic fears of invasion and espionage from Germany, prior to, and during, the First World War, it is unsurprising, given the history of Britain, that these fears existed. In addition, people living in the east of England believed that they would bear the brunt of any invasion. These threats, as we will see in the coming chapters, proved to be critical to the way the Government, as well as the public of the east of England, reacted to the fears of invasion and espionage during the First World War.

2

THE COMING OF THE HUN

Public and Governmental Fears of German Invasion and Espionage in the Years Before the Outbreak of War

ON 18 JANUARY 1871 UNDER A 'colourful forest' of military banners the German Empire was proclaimed in the magnificent Hall of Mirrors at the Palace of Versailles following the German confederation's triumphant victory over the French in the Franco-Prussian War under the 'Iron Chancellor' Otto von Bismarck. The separate Germanic kingdoms, duchies and states, bar Austria, had been united into a single Empire under the dominating hand of Prussia. The unification of the German states fundamentally shifted the balance of power in Europe and set the stage for the power struggles that would eventually lead Europe into two devastatingly cataclysmic conflicts.

Between German unification in 1870 and the outbreak of war in 1914 there developed an ever more intense rivalry between Germany and Britain, a rivalry which crossed all areas of life: ideological, political, diplomatic, technological, industrial, and economic. The noted historian Paul Kennedy notes that 'from the time of the Boer War onwards, it is possible to detect a growing British conviction that there existed a German threat'. Furthermore, this view was not just held by a suspicious but powerless public or 'right-wing journalists but also by influential figures in the navy, the army and the foreign office, by the crown, by significant members of the Liberal Party'.[1] Germanophobia was rooted both within the public sphere and the government. A deep mistrust grew between the two nations. This rivalry grew from a combination of factors such as Germany's ever growing economic and industrial output which seemed set to displace Britain's position as the leading economic and industrial powerhouse of Europe and indeed the world. Whilst economic and industrial rivalry gave the British government and public great cause for concern, the main area of British anxiety was the growing military strength of Germany and the increasing stridency of her imperial ambitions. From 1897 onwards, Germany under the leadership of the young ambitious and militaristic Kaiser Wilhelm II, began a naval building programme aimed at challenging Britain's dominance on the sea.

In Britain this naval construction was perceived as a direct and barely disguised threat to the defence of the home front and a challenge to Britain's status as the world's chief global power. How else, the accepted reasoning ran, were Berlin's policies to be interpreted?

However, the reality of Germany's foreign policy was more complicated, geared not so much as to overthrow and defeat

---

[1] P. Kennedy, *The Rise of the Anglo-German Antagonism, 1860-1914* (London: Allen and Unwin, 1982), p251

Britain but to cajole British policy into recognising and coming to terms with the reality of German power and its growing influence across the globe. Indeed, the naval arms race had as much to do, it could be argued, with strengthening German national pride and identity.[2]

The growing hostility between London and Berlin was exacerbated by Germany's political support for the Boers in the Second Boer War (1899-1902) and events such as the Moroccan Crisis of 1905 and 1906. The deterioration in Anglo-German relations pushed Britain into a military alliance with France. Which, in turn, fuelled German animosity towards Britain.

This rapid deepening of rivalries between the two powers convinced both the government and the public that Germany posed an existential threat to Britain and its interests. This sense of threat from direct military invasion and/or German spying was at its sharpest in the east of England.

Anti-espionage preparations began in 1909 when a sub-committee of the Committee of Imperial Defence was formed to discuss the extent of the spy threat and to organise Britain's response. The sub-committee concluded that German spies were indeed operating in Britain[3] and made four main recommendations for the government to act upon. The report highlighted first the need for the creation of a system in which to monitor foreign aliens in the country, secondly the creation of anti-sabotage plans for vulnerable areas such

---

[2] P. Padfield, *The Great Naval Race: The Anglo-German Naval Rivalry, 1900-1914* (London: Hart-Davis MacGibbon, 1974), Chapter 1

[3] 'Minutes of the third meeting of the sub-committee', 12 July 1909, PRO, Cab. 16/8.

as along the east coast, thirdly a broad extension of police powers to investigate foreign aliens within Britain suspected of espionage, and finally, and most importantly, the formation of a Secret Service to lead Britain's counter-espionage measures.[4] This indicates how seriously the threat was taken.

As a result of these recommendations two organisations were established to undertake counterespionage. These were the Secret Service Bureau which subsequently split to become MI5 and MI6. This consisted of a small group of army officers formed in 1909 under the command of the War Office. At the same time the Special Branch of the Criminal Investigation Department was set up under the direction of Scotland Yard.[5] A secret register of foreign aliens living in the United Kingdom was compiled. By 1913 it contained some 28,380 names, of which 11,100 were Germans. It is apparent that Germany was seen by the government as the biggest threat to British security.[6]

That a German invasion was feared, can be seen from the analysis undertaken by the Foreign Office in 1903. It was suggested that such an ambitious operation might be attempted with some 30,000 men. It was believed that foreign powers particularly Germany, would attempt raids along the eastern coast of Britain.[7] Significantly, the government

---

[4]'Report of a sub-committee', 24 July 1909, PRO, Cab. 16/8, 'Report of a sub-committee ...', CID paper 47-A

[5]N. Hiley, 'Counter Espionage and Security', pp635-636

[6]PRO, Cab. 17/90, CID paper 181B, appendix v, July 1913

[7]'Minutes of the meeting December 18 1903', PRO, Cab. 38/3/84

recognised eastern England as a particularly vulnerable area for invasion. At the same time, despite these findings, the government deemed invasion to be highly unlikely before a formal declaration of war between the two nations. However, the possibility could not be disregarded. It was agreed that in peacetime it would be impossible for Germany to prepare an invasion force without the government's prior knowledge, and that any threat would become clear to them if diplomatic measures failed.[8]

A sub-committee of the Committee of Imperial Defence concluded in 1908 that no large invasions were practical so long as British naval supremacy in the English Channel and North Sea (also named at the time as the German Sea) was maintained. If this supremacy were to be lost, it seemed that Britain would likely capitulate if a successful German landing was completed. As a consequence, it recommended that home defence forces should be strong enough both to repel small military raids and to ensure that any invading force must be so large that it could not elude the British fleet.[9] This committee met some 16 times between November 1907 and July 1908 and included such prominent members as Herbert Henry Asquith, the then Chancellor of the Exchequer and subsequently Prime Minister, David Lloyd George, later to be Chancellor of the Exchequer and Prime Minister, as well as Sir Edward Grey, the Secretary of State for Foreign Affairs. Their frequent meetings as well as its

---

[8]'Memorandum on the principles governing the defence of the United Kingdom', 4 October 1910, PRO, Cab. 38/16/20

[9]'Report and Proceedings', 22 October 1908, PRO, Cab. 16/3A

composition of senior government members suggest that the threat of an invasion was an extremely pressing issue. Their recommendations on home defence suggest that they believed that there was a fundamental inadequacy in Britain's defences. There was a significant enough threat of invasion to warrant the implementation of new defensive measures.[10]

The credibility of the public fear of Germany spying and invasion and evidence of pre-war apprehensions is best demonstrated through spy and invasion literature. This literature often featured Germany as the primary antagonist against Britain and became increasingly popular with the public in the late Victorian and Edwardian period. There are many examples of invasion-themed literature in Britain before the war. One of the most famous and important was *The Battle of Dorking* written in 1871 by George Tomkyns Chesney, detailing the destruction of the British channel fleet by the German Imperial Navy and a subsequent landing in southern England of some 200,000 Prussian soldiers.[11] This novel caused such a panic over the fear of German military aggression that the Prime Minister had to make a public speech reassuring a nervous public.[12] This novel kickstarted a wave of German-invasion literature such as *The Invasion of 1910* by William Le Queux in which Lowestoft was invaded by the Germans with the help of local sympathisers.[13] This

---

[10] 'Report and Proceedings of a sub CID Appointed by the Prime Minister to Reconsider the Question of Oversea Attack', 22 October 1908, PRO, Cab. 16/3A

[11] G. Chesney, *The Battle of Dorking* (Oxford: Oxford City Press, 2010)

[12] C. Pennel, 'The Germans Have Landed', p98

[13] W. Le Queux, *The Invasion of 1910* (London, 1906)

sold over one million copies showing the immense popularity of invasion literature with the pre-war British public. It helps to explain the development of more intense, localised fears within eastern England as it shocked specific areas such as small towns like Lowestoft.[14] Evidence for the development of localised fears can also be shown in 1909's *The Swoop of the Vulture* by James Blyth, where the Suffolk towns of Lowestoft and Great Yarmouth were invaded by German soldiers and aided also by local sympathisers.[15] These novels demonstrate a recurring theme – German sympathisers living within the local community. It helps to explain the intense suspicion the public in eastern England had during the war towards Germans living in the local area. The popularity of invasion literature in Britain before the war can be seen by the fact that out of the 317 texts on imaginary futures produced in the United Kingdom between 1871 and 1914, some 31 per cent concerned the themes of war and an onslaught on British soil.[16]

Spy literature was also extremely popular with the British public, such as William Le Queux's 1909 *Spies for the Kaiser*, which had been written with the intention to awaken the public and government to the inadequacies of British counterintelligence. It detailed how the east coast and London were swarming with spies. This book is another example of how local anxieties in eastern England developed. The

---

[14] C. Pennel, 'The Germans Have Landed', p98

[15] J. Blyth, *The Swoop of the Vulture* (London: Digby, Long and Company, 1909)

[16] C. Pennel, 'The Germans Have Landed', p98

emergence of spy literature certainly shows anxiety, even hysteria, about spies that existed in Britain years before the actual outbreak of hostilities. Adding to the volatile public mood was the fact that the authors of such novels such as William Le Queux used their writings as a way of voicing their genuine fears to a mass audience, in the hope of pressurising the government to prepare for the oncoming German threat. Millions of readers were alarmed, their fears stoked by the torrent of spy literature. Following the publication of his novel *Spies for the Kaiser*, William Le Queux found himself inundated with letters from the public reporting suspicious Germans living around important infrastructure on the east coast and in London. Public concern about German espionage can also be seen by the frequent press reports on the existence of active spy rings and fifth columnists. In 1907 the *Morning Post* published a letter claiming that 90,000 spies and German army reservists were living in Britain. A Bath newspaper reported that there existed 50,000 stands of Mauser rifles stored near Charing Cross Station, in addition to around 60,000 German reservists living in the capital ready to use them. These claims are laughable considering there were only 50,000 Germans living in Britain in the years prior to the war.[17] The atmosphere of suspicion and distrust towards outsiders was legitimatised and made even more prevalent by the British press. The historian David French noted that as well as spy literature and the press stoking public fears, German military

---

[17] D.French, 'Spy Fever in Britain, 1900-1915', *The Historical Journal*, Vol 21, No 2 (June, 1978)

activities in the late 19th century and early 20th century lent credibility to these fears. According to French, fears reached 'fever pitch'[18] between 1908 and 1909. In 1911 the local *Lowestoft Journal* reported on the formation of a National Service Association. It discussed the threat of a German invasion and the inadequacies of Britain's defences, in which the writer calls for national service to defend the country. The reality of anxieties about a German invasion in the east of England in the pre-war years is demonstrable.[19]

Fears of invasion and espionage were evident at every level of British society. The public and government perceived the growing strength of Germany as a clear and looming military threat. The government took seriously enough the threat of invasion by Germany. Germany's increased military preparations were alarming but did not necessarily suggest that this was as yet perceived as an *imminent* threat to Britain. What we can see, however, is that the east of England was considered particularly vulnerable and a likely place for both small raids and a full-scale invasion. Furthermore, Germany was considered by the British government the most likely power to attempt either of these. In respect of espionage, the government perceived German spying to be a not only significant threat to the nation but that the threat was already serious enough to greatly increase counter-espionage preparations. For the public, the literature concerning the

---

[18] D. French, 'Spy Fever', p358

[19] 'As to National Service', 20 August 1910, *The Lowestoft Journal*, p4

invasion of Britain and the threat of espionage show that these fears were high within the public's mind before the Great War. It was seen to be fundamentally as a German threat.

Edward VII (King of Great Britain and Ireland, 1901-1910) and Wilhelm II (German Emperor, 1888-1918). Despite the two monarchs ruling over countries increasingly at odds with one another, they were related through Queen Victoria who was the mother of Edward VII and the grandmother of Wilhelm II.

Kaiser Wilhelm I (First Emperor of the unified German Empire, 1871-1888).

Otto von Bismarck, Chancellor of the German Empire (1871-1890) and architect of German unification. As Chancellor, Bismarck played a key role in the growing strength of the German Empire. However, he was dismissed by the new Emperor, Wilhelm II in 1890.

Cartoon depicting five nations involved in the naval arms race (Puck magazine, 1909).

Alfred von Tirpitz (State Secretary of the German Imperial Naval Office, (1897-1916). As the leading figure in the Imperial, Navy von Tirpitz played a vital role in the growth of the Navy which did much to fuel the growing animosity between the United Kingdom and Germany.

The Anglo-German naval arms race was central to the growing mistrust between Germany and the United Kingdom in the late 19th and early 20th centuries.

GERMAN NAVAL ESTIMATES.

The German Naval Estimates for 1904 make provision, we learn, for the construction of two battleships, three large cruisers, three second-class cruisers, and three torpedo-boats at a total cost of just under 108,000,000 marks, an increase on the current year of 3,500,000 marks. The standing service of the Navy and coast defence requirements is down for nearly 100,000,000 marks, or 6,500,000 marks more than in 1903. A further sum of 26,000,000 marks is allotted for coaling stations and the protection of German colonies, this amount being also an advance on previous estimates by over 2,000,000 marks.

GERMAN NAVAL CONSTRUCTION.

THE KAISER AND THE EVOLUTION OF ARMAMENTS.

BERLIN, November 18. — The German Emperor attended the third general meeting of the Society of Naval Engineers, which was held this morning in the Technical School at Charlottenburg. Among other prominent persons present was Admiral Von Tirpitz, Secretary of State for the Imperial Navy. A paper was read upon the development in the manner of placing heavy guns on battleships and its effect upon the design and construction of such vessels. In the discussion which followed the Emperor took part.

Arthur James Balfour, First Earl of Balfour (Prime Minister of the United Kingdom 1902-1905).

Herbert Henry Asquith, First Earl of Oxford and Asquith (Prime Minister of the United Kingdom, 1908-1916).

Front cover of the 1871 pamphlet edition of *The Battle of Dorking* by George Tomkyns Chesney.

William Tufnell Le Queux. One of the most active, prolific, successful and influential authors in the invasion genre in the United Kingdom, Le Queux was famous for his books including *The Invasion of 1910* and *Spies of the Kaiser*.

3

THE INVASION OF EASTERN ENGLAND

Government and Military Reactions to the Fears of a German Invasion in the East of England

TO WHAT EXTENT DID GOVERNMENT COUNTER-invasion preparations following the outbreak of the Great War reflect a genuine fear of a potential invasion within the British government? And how was public life in eastern England affected?

Following the declaration of war with Germany on 4 August 1914 senior Ministers met to consider the possible threat of an invasion. On 7 October, in what would be the first wartime meeting of the Committee of Imperial Defence, debate was dedicated entirely to the topic of invasion. In this meeting, and the many subsequent meetings that followed, there were disagreements within government circles as to the potential size of an invading force. Lord Kitchener, the Secretary of State for War, for example, suggested that anywhere between 70,000 and 200,000 German soldiers could attempt an invasion. Kitchener believed Germany had the military capability to create and organise such an invasion force, a notion which was supported by other members such as the Foreign Secretary, Sir Edward Grey. However, Winston Churchill, the First Lord of the Admiralty, believed Kitchener's figures to be impractical and that more realistically Germany would carry out smaller raids upon the coast of Britain by up to no more than 30,000 men. Despite these disagreements amongst committee members, it is clear that the numbers they conceived had far risen substantially from their estimates in 1903. The government, as well as considering the potential size of an invading force, also discussed the practicality of such an invasion by the German military. Kitchener argued that at the war's current stage of mobility the Germans would be foolish to attempt an invasion. However, if the expected deadlock and stalemate between the Allies and the Germans were to occur then there was a serious risk of an attempted invasion. This position was supported by, amongst others, Sir Edward Grey. The government whilst not immediately concerned with a serious threat of invasion from the outset of the war, foresaw invasion as considerably more likely if the western front ground down into a state of deadlock. There was not agreement about this across government. Maurice Hankey, the Secretary to the Committee of Imperial Defence, noted many years after the war:

> At the beginning of September, when we were tuning up our plans for home defence the situation on the Continent was certainly one of almost unrelieved gloom. Who then could say that the Government was wrong in keeping a vigilant eye on home defence? Suppose the French Army had been encircled, as might well have happened! Suppose France had collapsed, as in 1870 and later in 1940! What would then have been our position

with the whole coast of France and Belgium in Germany's hands? Invasion, though still difficult, would have been appreciably nearer.

This telling recollection from Hankey summarises the position in which the government found itself in late 1914. It was a situation filled with paranoia, anxiety and uncertainty over the future of British home defence. The government was divided both upon the issue of when an invasion might come, and not knowing if Britain was safe from the threat of invasion. Finally, the government also discussed the likely landing locations of a potential invasion force. The general staff of the British armed forces all agreed that any invasion would be impractical for the Germans to attempt along the English Channel. Therefore, any landings would have to be made north of the river Thames, yet close enough to the capital. East Anglia was considered by the British government and the military to be the most likely location for invasion.[1] This is reinforced by a government-issued civilian guidance poster for Suffolk which quoted that 'the Norfolk and Suffolk coast line is the most likely objective' of an invading force.[2] Nearly half of all the documents dealing with invasion were created between September and December of 1914.[3] There

---

[1] 'Minutes of the 129th meeting of the CID', 7 October 1914, PRO, Cab. 38/28/47

[2] 'Guidance to the civil population of East Suffolk in the event of a landing by the enemy on the coast', in St Edmundsbury Local History <http://www.stedmundsburychronicle.co.uk>

[3] H.R. Moon, 'The Invasion of the United Kingdom: Public Controversy and Official Planning, 1888-1918' (PhD Thesis, University of London, 1968), p535

was a sense of urgency about these plans – it suggests also that later plans were modifications.

It became clear to the government that there needed to be contingency plans should there be German raids or even an invasion. Both possibilities required organisation both at local and central government levels. The historian Grieves, noted 'the threat of invasion required a chain of command ... which linked the government, army, lord lieutenants, magistrates and police'.[4] In response the Home Secretary, Reginald McKenna, in November 1914 ordered the eastern and southern coastal county Lord Lieutenants to form both central and local emergency committees to organise local responses to the threat of invasion. The main tasks of these emergency committees were chiefly to assist the military and government in: the prevention of invasion, keeping troops mobile, organising entrenchment and other minor defensive construction, organising civilian armed resistance, and finally, the organisation of civilian evacuation.[5] The government was particularly worried that these emergency committees would panic an already nervous public, and thus a balance was needed to be struck between relaying crucial information to the public and causing unnecessary alarm. Even as late as July 1915, the Home Secretary Reginald McKenna warned 'they [local emergency committees] should avoid any action or statement likely to cause alarm or panic'.[6]

These committees included central emergency committees

---

[4]Pennel, 'The Germans Have Landed', p104

[5]Ibid

[6]HC Parliamentary Debate, 26 July 1915, 73, col. 1930-8

on a regional county level such as Norfolk or Essex, which, in turn, controlled local emergency committees representing towns and villages. County level committees were under the strict control of the Home Office which worked with the military and the Lords Lieutenants of the counties. The Home Secretary summarised the organization of these committees: 'The government laid down certain general instructions ... and the committees carry them out under the supervision of the Lord Lieutenant, who is assisted in each county by a central organising committee, on which the military authorities are also represented'.[7] The historian, Edwin A. Pratt, elaborated on the Home Secretary's explanation, noting that the committees consisted of well-trusted members of the local community as well as local military commanders. Local citizens were also sworn in as special police constables to undertake various public duties. They would possess the powers of regular police officers in emergencies. Many people in the east of England volunteered. For example, Norwich had 900 special constables in its executive force by 1917.[8] In the event of an attempted raid or invasion the chief of police who sat on the emergency committees and his police officers would be responsible for the guidance of the civilian population and would work under instructions issued by the military.[9]

The main duties of the emergency committees were spelled out by the Home Secretary who stated that 'their chief duty

[7] Ibid

[8] Edwin A. Pratt, *British Railways in the Great War*, pp827-828

[9] Ibid

is ... to organise the action to be taken by the civil population in the event of a hostile landing'.[10] This entailed both the organisation of various emergency schemes as well as relaying the government's and military's official information to the public. General instructions issued by the military and government were universal and were followed by all emergency committees. At the local level emergency committees organised their own emergency schemes relevant to their local area, with the Home Secretary adding that 'In view of the varying conditions in each locality the details of the arrangements are necessarily left to the local military authorities and the committees'.[11]

Pratt elaborated on the Home Secretary's proposals detailing how the emergency committees were tasked with the compilation of inventories of items which were deemed to be useful to the military. Police and civilians in the event of an invasion would destroy these items if they could not be utilised. This was to ensure that equipment did not fall into the hands of an invading force. These inventories included numbers and locations of goods such as: livestock, various tools, building supplies, vehicles, weapons, defensive materials, and food supplies.[12]

Emergency committees in the event of invasion would also be responsible for organising and directing working parties of local residents who, supplied with tools, would assist the military and police in tasks such as blocking roads, evacuating

---

[10]HC Parliamentary Debate, 26 July 1915, 73, col. 1930-8

[11]Ibid

[12]Pratt, *British Railways*, p828

livestock or felling trees. In the case of Norwich there were eight such working parties who were ready to undertake these duties should the situation arise.[13] Prior to the outbreak of war, governmental preparations were a largely national affair, and were confined mainly to coastal defences. When war broke out preparations were devolved due to the increase in the scale of organisation required. Inclusion of civilians to these anti-invasion preparations meant that home defence was not any longer a government concern to be organised by the government and the military but was now a civilian concern. The fact that the government believed that these instructions should be made public, demonstrates that the assessment of the risk of invasion had clearly and dramatically increased.

In the event of an attempt at invasion, one of the most important duties of emergency committees was the organisation of civilian evacuation. If this happened the public would be alerted to the danger through ringing of church bells and would be instructed to take with them only clothes, blankets and enough food and drink to last for 48 hours. Civilians would then evacuate via agreed routes.[14] Also, in the event of an attempted invasion, martial law would be declared. Emergency committees following government edicts, would instruct civilians to, whenever possible, remain in their own homes unless the order was

---

[13] Pratt, *British Railways*, p829

[14] 'In Case of Invasion', 25 December 1914, *Chelmsford Chronicle*, p4

given to evacuate.[15] The central emergency committees had, since the outbreak of war, also been working on large scale evacuation routes for civilians to follow. For example, in counties in the east of England civilians were instructed to head away from the coast towards Oxfordshire. Meanwhile, local emergency committees had already planned local evacuation routes and had distributed maps and posters to the public detailing those routes.[16] One person living in Essex at the time even recalled arrows painted onto the trees to mark these routes in the village of Stock, which highlights how the threat of invasion was a constant visual reminder for people living in the east of England.[17] Emergency committees, as mentioned earlier, had created detailed inventories of all the various vehicles and wagons that could be used to assist civilian evacuation. All those who were able to drive, motor vehicles and garages as well as quantities and types of spares, had to be registered with the local emergency committees. In Norwich, for example, some 200 cars and 300 drivers were registered who could assist with civilian evacuation in the event of an invasion. 100 mechanics were also registered so that they could disable abandoned vehicles so they could not be used by an invading force.[18]

---

[15]'City of Norwich Instructions for the Guidance of the Civil Population in the Event of a Landing by the Enemy in this County' in E.A. Pratt, *British Railways and the Great War* (London, Selwyn and Blout Ltd, 1921), p830

[16]'Dunmow District Emergency Instructions', in Essex Voices Past, http://www.essexvoicespast.com> [accessed 20 March 2019]

[17]Pennel, *'The Germans Have Landed'*, p110

[18]S. Browning, *Norfolk Coast in the Great War: King's Lynn, Hunstanton, Sherringham, Cromer and Great Yarmouth* (Barnsley: Pen and Sword Military, 2017), pp43-44

Emergency committees would instruct the public which roads would be required by the military. The police would, as far as possible, manage what roads were needed. Police were to instruct civilians to leave these roads immediately if the military were approaching.[19][20] The government also decided that there would be no provisions made to evacuate civilians from the east of England by rail, as rail lines would be overstretched owing to the needs of the military. The Great Eastern Railway which served eastern England, for example, mostly consisted of single-track lines thus making it impractical for civilian evacuation as there would need to be a constant stream of military transportation to the coast.[21] Extensive evacuation plans drawn up by the government, as well as by central and local emergency committees, further demonstrates the government's heightened fear of invasion. There were no government evacuation plans for civilians before the outbreak of war and certainly nothing to the extent of the rigorous planning seen in the emergency committees.

Government and emergency committees also made plans for the destruction of property in the event of an invasion. There were strict regulations on how this was to be implemented. The committees listed four main categories of property that would either be evacuated or, if evacuation was not possible, destroyed. The four main categories detailed by the government and emergency committees were:

---

[19] 'City of Norwich Emergency Committee Instructions'

[20] 'In Case of Invasion', 25 December 1914, in *Chelmsford Chronicle*, p4

[21] Pratt, *British Railways*, p826

items of transport, tools, public infrastructure, and, finally, food and livestock. One of the main threats for an invading force was that its supply lines would run out before the completion of its military objectives. Hence the removal or destruction of transport and facilities which would aid German supply lines, was highly prioritised. Transport – which included animals – were to be taken to designated assembly points to await further military instructions. Anything that could not be moved was to be destroyed under military or police supervision. The government ordered that there was to be no public destruction of infrastructure such as bridges or telegraph lines, for example, unless given direct instructions by the military authorities.[22] It was the government's belief that the widespread unorganised destruction of vital infrastructure would cause havoc to the mobility and coordination of the home defence forces. Instead, government and the military believed infrastructure should only be destroyed if it faced an imminent threat of being used by an invading force. Tools were also deemed to be extremely important, and so all tools were to be handed in at designated collection points. Work gangs under military supervision, would await instructions on how to employ these tools in projects. Tools would otherwise be destroyed preventing them from falling into enemy hands.[23] Food and livestock were likely to be the one most useful to an invading

---

[22]'City of Norwich Emergency Committee Instructions'

[23]'Borough of Dover Emergency Committee Poster on Evacuation Plans', in E.A. Pratt, *British Railways and the Great War* (London, Selwyn and Blout Ltd, 1921), p837

force. Accordingly, in the event of an invasion, any cattle or food stores were to be evacuated immediately. Otherwise, if they could not be successfully evacuated, they were to be destroyed, however, similarly to public infrastructure, this was only to be carried out under military authorisation. The government had plans to compensate those who had to destroy their property. However, anyone resisting military-ordered destruction would be ineligible to claim this compensation.[24] It is clear that civilians were essential to the government's anti-invasion strategy and would play a significant role in the destruction of vital property.

The government considered whether to establish volunteer defence forces which had been increasingly supported by the public following the German invasion of Belgium in August 1914. In September of 1914 a letter was published by the *Cambridge Independent* newspaper arguing that every able-bodied man needed to be armed and ready to resist invading forces, noting how Belgian civilians had been defenceless during the invasion.[25] There are further demonstrations of public approval in the east of England's support for volunteer defence forces. For example, in November 1914 the chairman of the Witham local emergency committee in Essex argued that both men and women should join the fight for resistance,[26] as well as a letter published in the *Chronicle* newspaper stating that civilians would 'rather die rifle in

---

[24]'City of Norwich Emergency Committee Instructions'

[25]'Letter to the Editor', 25 September 1914, *Cambridge Independent Press*, p4

[26]*Essex County Standard*, 7 November 1914, p8

hand'.[27] The extreme expressions of support for public resistance demonstrate clearly that in eastern England the threat of invasion was taken very seriously by the local population. Despite these examples of public support, there is also evidence that this was not universally popular. A letter in *The Times* suggested that volunteer forces would lead to reprisals from the invading forces in the form of 'blazing villages, brutal executions, and all the nameless horrors' that had been recorded during the invasion of Belgium.[28] Government and military authorities were also highly nervous about the prospect of unregulated groups of armed civilians.

In response, in November 1914 the government approved the creation of the Volunteer Training Corps. This was an extremely popular move with the public and by 1915 there was estimated to be some 1,500 such groups across the country.[29] It was stated that no unofficial organisations would be recognised to partake in armed defence, and would have to surrender any arms or equipment.[30] It was stressed that unregulated armed defence could provoke reprisals from the enemy.[31] The Volunteer Training Corps consisted of men over the age of service or those who had been exempt from active service. Their duties were to guard and patrol areas vulnerable to raids or invasion as well as other militarily

---

[27] *Chronicle*, 6 November 1914, p5

[28] *The Times*, 17 August 1914, p9

[29] 'Volunteer Training Corps', 23 July 1915, *Diss Express*, p5

[30] Ibid

[31] 'In Case of a Raid', 5 December 1914, *Essex Newsman*, p1

important locations. In the event of invasion, the Volunteer Training Corps were to assist the regular defence forces who would provide the main resistance to German forces. The main enthusiasm for the Volunteer Training Corps was found in the early years of the war. For example, in June 1915 there were some 590,000 volunteers which had decreased to some 285,000 by February 1918.[32] This could reflect both the government's and the public's decreasing fear of an invasion as the war progressed. It is just as likely that conscription and the widening criteria for army recruitment in the later years of the war had an effect. Whilst nationally the Volunteer Training Corps saw a decline in its membership as the war went on, in Essex the number of volunteer forces increased, rising from some 2,000 volunteers to 5,000 by late 1916, indicating that fear of an invasion was more prevalent in the east of England.[33]

The Volunteer Training Corps was not the only volunteer movement used in civil defence. The Scouts, for example, mapped out land for the military and emergency committees as well as patrolling vulnerable areas such as vital communication lines[34] or bridges for example.[35] On the coast and in high invasion risk counties such as those on the east of England, a secret list of observers was established by

---

[32]Ian F. Beckett, *A Nation in Arms: The British Army in the First World War* (Pen and Sword Military), pp15-16

[33]'Essex Volunteer Force', *Chelmsford Chronicle*, 13 October 1916, p5

[34]*Essex County Standard*, 22 August 1914, p4

[35]Joe Cook, August 1914, in Pennel, 'The Germans Have Landed', p105

government officials. They would observe the coast for signs of invasion and would aid in raising the alarm, if needed. Owing to the sensitive nature of this work and the vital importance of this task, there was a need for absolute secrecy. Accordingly, those chosen to be observers were deemed to be highly trustworthy members of the local community.[36]

Fishermen along the east coast of England were also employed by the government under the Royal Naval Reserve Trawler Section and were employed in tasks such as patrolling the sea for German naval ships, as well as the highly dangerous task of minesweeping. In East Anglia many fishermen volunteered. In the towns of Great Yarmouth and Lowestoft alone some 500 ships were employed.[37] This work was, of course, highly dangerous with many fishing vessels being sunk by German submarines.[38] Similarly to the Volunteer Training Corps the vast numbers of civilians in the east of England who volunteered for dangerous roles in civil defence highlights that the public took seriously the threat of an invasion on the eastern coast.

There were sufficient apprehensions at government level that a German invasion of the east of England might be attempted. This built upon a pre-existing belief that such an invasion was to an extent probable. What was new, was the inclusion of the public into the government's home defence plans for the first time since the Napoleonic Wars. This

---

[36] Browning, *Norfolk Coast*, p49

[37] Browning, *Norfolk Coast*, p49

[38] 'Sunk by Mine', *Diss Express*, 11 September 1914

materially affected the lives of the residential population either directly through participation in the various largely civilian bodies engaged in home defence, or indirectly by living in an ethos of threats and fears as well as restrictions to individual freedoms.

Maurice Pascal Alers Hankey (First Baron Hankey), Secretary to the Committee of Imperial Defence 1912-1938. Hankey played a vital role in the organisation of Home Defence in the years during and preceding the war.

Field Marshall Horatio Herbert Kitchener (First Earl Kitchener). Member of the Committee of Imperial Defence and Secretary of State for War 1914-1916.

> **NOTE.**—The Revised Instructions dated 1st March, 1916, are cancelled and are to be destroyed.
>
> ## COUNTY OF EAST SUFFOLK
> (Inclusive of the Borough of Lowestoft).
>
> # NEW INSTRUCTIONS
> For the Guidance of the Civil Population in the event of a Landing by the Enemy on the Coast.
>
> **1st JANUARY, 1917.**
>
> **To be read over carefully and kept for ready reference.**
>
> 1. **PRELIMINARY.**—It is of great importance that the public should realise that the success of all measures for their protection and the defeat of the enemy depends on their own hearty co-operation. They should, therefore, understand that—
>
>   (a) A hostile landing is no more likely now than in the previous stages of the War, but it is **possible.** If contemplated by the enemy, the Norfolk and Suffolk coast line is the most likely objective, being the nearest to the German ports and for other reasons. It is necessary, therefore, to be thoroughly prepared.
>
>   (b) If a hostile landing takes place it is vitally important that the enemy should be denied **Transport and Petrol,** by its being removed inland, rendered useless, or destroyed, before he is able to occupy any portion of territory. This is the work for which the Civil Population is responsible.
>
>   (c) A county organisation has been established during the War (by Emergency Committees sitting at the various Police Divisional Headquarters), for dealing with the above measures for removal, rendering useless, or destruction.

Guidance to the civil population of East Suffolk in the event of a landing by the enemy on the coast.

Reginald McKenna, Home Secretary 1911-1915. McKenna established the emergency committees to organise local populations in the event of German invasion.

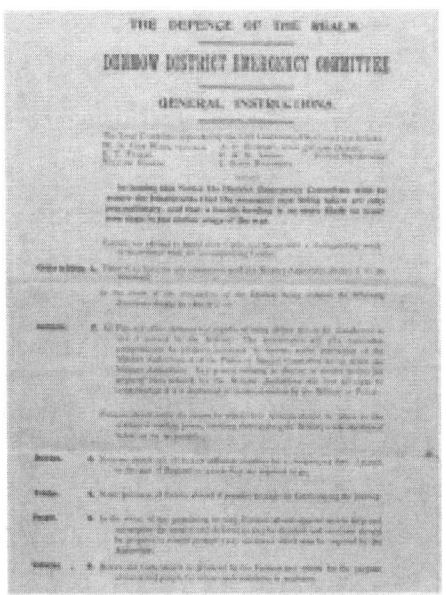
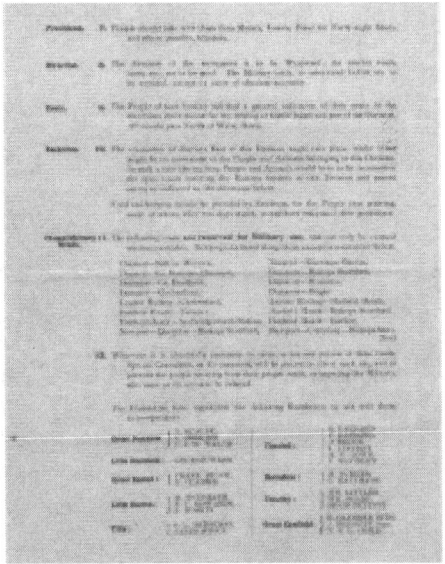

Dunmow District Emergency Instructions. One of the many detailed home defence instructions issued by the emergency committees on the direction of the Home Office to those living in the east of England.

Official uniforms of the Volunteer Training Corps, published in February 1915.

Official badge of the Volunteer Training Corps.

Trumpington Volunteer Training Corps, November 1915. Founded in November 1914, the Volunteer Training Corps that sprang up across the east of England was a direct response to the fear many felt towards the prospect of an invasion and serve as proof that the fear of invasion was one felt seriously by the local population during the First World War.

South Benfleet Special Police Constables. Photograph taken some time near the end of the war. On 27 August 1914 the Special Constables Act 1914 passed through parliament and gained royal assent the following day. The act allowed for those unable to join the armed forces to become Special Police Constables who would have the same temporary powers as the regular police forces.

4

ENEMIES ON OUR DOORSTEP?

Government and Military Reactions to the Fears of German Espionage in the East of England

HOW MUCH DID GOVERNMENT TAKE SERIOUSLY the threat of espionage? What measures were put in place to counteract espionage and to what extent did these measures affect on the people living in the East of England?

Legislation formed the backbone of the government's anti-espionage strategy during the First World War and proved to be a decisive factor in the fight against German intelligence. Vast arrays of legislation were implemented by the government during the Great War to combat the threat of espionage. The most important and influential piece of legislation was the Defence of the Realm Act 1914. The Defence of the Realm Act, better known by its acronym DORA, was an emergency piece of legislation deemed so urgently necessary by the government and military authorities that it was rushed through parliament only four days after the declaration of war in August 1914. There was not even a debate by MPs. DORA gave the government unprecedented powers to make regulations. This included provisions to prevent spies, saboteurs and fifth columnists from: communicating information to the enemy, obtaining information which could assist the enemy in its war effort against the United Kingdom and her allies – and to secure the safety of vital infrastructure such as communication lines and facilities, transportation networks and structures such as railway lines, roads, bridges, as well as shipping facilities such as harbours or docks. DORA allowed for those charged with breaching regulations to be tried via a military court martial[1]. This underlines the government's profound fear of espionage. It is constitutionally controversial, and it even suggests the government did not trust the judiciary to deal with these trials effectively.

DORA was revised and amended many times by parliament throughout the duration of the war and by the end of hostilities in 1918 contained a vast array of regulations aimed at countering the threats posed by espionage. Information on the ever-growing list of criminal offences was relayed to the public via the police and the local emergency committees through posters and pamphlets. One such poster detailed how it was an offence for citizens to: collect, or attempt to collect, information deemed useful to the enemy, interfere with telegraph lines, own any telegraphic devices without the permission of the police, trespass on railway lines or bridges, approach bases of military/naval importance without the permission of the military authorities,

---

[1] 'DORA 1914, Chapter 29', in Legislation.Gov.UK <http://www.legislation.gov.uk/ukpga/Geo5/4-5/29/contents/enacted> [accessed 1 April 2019]

photograph/sketch areas of military importance – as well as seemingly trivial regulations such as forbidding the ownership of homing pigeons or displaying bonfires or fireworks without the permission of the police.[2] These are just some of the regulations listed by the government. This list demonstrates how all matters of life had been altered and affected by the government's fear of espionage. DORA simultaneously greatly extended the powers of the police and military authorities. It permitted them the authority to: forcibly remove inhabitants from certain areas deemed important to the military, enter and search properties at any given time, seize or destroy any property which infringed upon DORA regulations, stop and search any vehicle and arrest without a warrant any person suspected of breaching or intending to breach DORA regulations.[3] This extension of powers of police forces and military/naval authorities, demonstrates the government's concerns about German espionage. The government was willing to cast aside basic and fundamental civil liberties enshrined through centuries of common law. An example is the need for an arrest warrant, which was no longer required. Whilst many regulations such as those prohibiting the collection of information deemed useful to the enemy, or prohibiting the interference of telegraph lines, etc, are to be expected in a time of war, regulations against trivial offences such as

---

[2]'Poster on DORA Regulations, issued 1914' in National Archives <http://www.nationalarchives.gov.uk> [accessed 1 April 2019]

[3]'DORA poster on Naval and Military powers, issued 1914', in National Archives <http://www.nationalarchives.gov.uk> [accessed 1 April 2019]

owning homing pigeons or lighting bonfires and fireworks without permission, highlights the government's anxiety and demonstrates its perception of the gravity of the situation.

Many legal cases illustrate the great implications DORA had for those living in the east of England. There were many convictions and arrests due to the breach of regulations, many of which contained little evidence of foul play being involved or intended. Some of the more seemingly trivial regulations resulted in financial charges. For example, in 1915 an Essex man was arrested and fined £1 for lighting a bonfire without the permission of the authorities despite there being no signs of ill intention.[4] There are also incidents of people convicted of acts considered to aid the enemy, such as in 1915 where a man in the Suffolk village of Framlingham was convicted under DORA for publishing pamphlets of guided scenic tours around the local area. These, however, contained information relating to the disposition of troops and ships which he claimed was well-known public information. The court ruled that information could not be published by British citizens regardless of their public knowledge and was fined £10.[5] Similarly, Peter Kilmonock of Stratford was fined the then huge sum of £35 under the Act in 1918 over materials deemed by the military authorities as damaging to the war effort.[6] Living in the vicinity of certain areas of military or naval importance could have severe consequences for those

---

[4]'A Costly Fire', *Essex Newsman*, 30 October 1915, p3

[5]'Defence of the Realm Act', *Framlingham Weekly News*, 17 July 1915, p1

[6]*Essex Newsman*, 20 April 1918, p3

who breached regulations. For example, in 1914 a Chelmsford man was arrested and removed from Essex after he was accused of loitering near an ammunition store, again despite showing no intention of acting with ill intent.[7] Similarly, in Lawford, a man was arrested for loitering near a waterworks and was accused of using a flashlight to send signals, which, according to the *Chelmsford Chronicle*, was yet to be proven.[8]

Another crucial and controversial piece of legislation issued by the government, was the Aliens Restriction Act of 1914, which had consequences for those living in the east of England. It aimed at controlling the movements of foreign nationals living in Britain. The Act declared that: any 'enemy aliens' not of military age had until 10 August to leave the country, otherwise they would have to register themselves with the police. However, if they chose to remain in the United Kingdom, they were forbidden under the Act to move more than 5 miles from their homes and could not live on the east coast or near any naval or military bases.[9] The extreme and xenophobic measures of this Act further highlight the government's fear of German espionage and demonstrates how far it was willing to go to counter this threat. The fact that these regulations applied to all foreign nationals also indicates the extent of governmental paranoia.

---

[7] 'Defence of the Realm – An Arrest at Chelmsford', *Essex Newsman*, 14 November 1914, p3

[8] 'Manningtree Man Charged', *Chelmsford Chronicle*, 13 November 1914, p2

[9] 'Minutes of the 125th meeting of the CID', 3 March 1914, PRO, Cab. 2/3, 4 & 5 Geo. 5, c. 12

It might be assumed that such measures would apply only to those from nations at war with Britain. The Act had an explicit and harsh effect on those living on the east coast. Foreign nationals whose families may have resided there for generations could no longer live there. The east of England, owing to its vulnerable coastline was considered a prime target for any potential landing. There were many areas of military and naval importance – which in turn further decreased the area in which foreign nationals could live and work.

The passing of the Aliens Restriction Act in 1914 led swiftly to a series of mass arrests of foreign nationals. By 28 September 6,700 Germans had been arrested.[10] These numbers increased rapidly as the year went on and by 1 May 1915 some 20,000 civilians had been detained on government orders.[11] Upon the outbreak of war the British government and General Staff of the Armed Forces had decided it was necessary, owing to the threat of espionage, for the immediate internment of all Germans between the ages of 17 and 42. However, this decision was reversed the very next day to apply only to those deemed a potential threat to Britain's national security. It shows the widespread level of apprehension within the government and military authorities. Even though it was short lived, it would have been the biggest series of mass arrests and imprisonment in British history.

---

[10] 'Internment of enemy aliens', R. McKenna, 7 December 1914, PRO, Cab. 37/122/182

[11] P. Panayi, *Prisoners of Britain: German Civilian and Combatant Internees During the First World War* (Manchester University Press, 2012), p44

However, this initial period of rationality did not last. The British ocean liner *The Lusitania* was sunk by a German U-boat U-20 in May 1915 and 1,198 civilians died. Demands from the public and MPs followed for whole-scale internment of German nationals and descendants. On 11 May 1915 a mass demonstration and march from the City of London to the House of Commons took place petitioning for full-scale internment. There were two petitions each containing approximately 250,000 signatures[12] – an indicator of the depth of public fury and fear over the possibility of German agents operating in Britain. Anger in Britain against Germans reached its boiling point in the aftermath of *The Lusitania* tragedy. Riots broke out across the country. Countless German-owned or German-run businesses were destroyed by rampaging mobs. The anger and thirst for revenge drove many more young men to enlist in the war against Germany. The novelist and poet, D.H. Lawrence, went so far as to say that 'I am mad with rage myself. I would like to kill a million Germans – two millions'[13]. The bitterness and rage that engulfed the British people left a legacy of hatred towards Germans living in the country that lasted well after the conclusion of hostilities. Lawrence later wrote that 'a wave of criminal lust rose and possessed England' kickstarting a 'reign of terror' in which the British public abandoned its 'sense of truth, of justice and of human honour'.[14] Public

---

[12] 'The Annual Register', *The Times*, 10, 11 and 13 May 1915, p103

[13] D.H. Lawrence, *Selected Letters* (Harmondsworth, 1978), p83

[14] D.H. Lawrence, *Kangaroo* (1923, reprinted Harmondsworth, 1985), pp235-6

pressure eventually forced the Prime Minister, Herbert Asquith, to begin the process of whole-scale internment of Germans living in Britain from 13 May 1915 onwards. By the end of the war, there were over 24,000 German civilians interned in Britain,[15]. The German community in Britain, which had in 1914 numbered approximately 57,000 people, had shrunk dramatically to 22,000.[16]

The Aliens Restriction Act produced many cases of extreme hardship and humiliation for those living within the east of England. There are countless cases of citizens being fined for very minor incidents, such as a German in Stratford named Harieg Reeg who was fined £100 in August 1914 for failing to notify the police that he was changing his address, an enormous sum for the time.[17] Similarly, Frederick Specht, who lived in the port town of Harwich in Essex, was charged with harbouring an unregistered alien after he failed to register his wife with the police, despite having registered himself. The pair were each fined £5 despite both having lived in England for 39 years.[18] The Act did not just have consequences for those who failed to register either themselves or their address, but also had consequences for foreign

---

[15] P. Panayi, *Prisoners of Britain: German Civilian and Combatant Internees During the First World War* (Manchester University Press, 2012), p44

[16] P. Panayi, *Prisoners of Britain: German Civilian and Combatant Internees During the First World War* (Manchester University Press, 2012), p2

[17] 'German fined £100', *Chelmsford Chronicle*, 28 August 1914, p2

[18] 'Alien Fined for Harbouring his Wife', *Chelmsford Chronicle*, 28 August 1914, p2

nationals in the east of England who owned or operated transport vehicles. Phillip Schier from Leigh-on-Sea, Essex, was arrested for owning two motor cars which he had failed to register with the police. He had lived in the United Kingdom for 15 years without any legal trouble with the authorities and claimed he had been unaware of the need to register motor vehicles. As a result of his actions Schier was subsequently threatened with three months' imprisonment unless he paid an eye-watering fine of £150.[19] Events such as these were a common experience for Germans and other foreign nationals living in the east of England at the time. As the war continued, they faced increasing surveillance and restriction. Government measures had severe and profound repercussions for those under suspicion, whether of a practical nature such as freedom of movement and employment but also of a psychological one – the burden of being a hated and mistrusted outsider.

Easily the largest, most glaring and long-lasting legacy of the government's anti-espionage measures was the rapid development of British spy agencies in terms of size, organisation and duties. Employment within these agencies grew quickly following the declaration of war. The staff of the Security Service grew from just 19 in August 1914 to 844 by November 1914.[20] This unprecedented increase of staff in the space of a mere four months signifies the growing importance the Security Service had in counterespionage. It

---

[19] 'An Alien's Motor Car', *Essex Newsman*, 29 August 1914, p2

[20] N. Hiley, 'Counter Espionage and Security in Great Britain During the First World War', *The English Historical Review*, Vol 101, No 400 (July,1986), p667, Appendix B

is indicative of the depth of government alarm about potential German espionage. Establishment of an effective counter-intelligence service grew higher and higher on the order of government priorities. The nature and expansion of the secret services would have been unimaginable even in the suspicion-tinged years before the war.

The Security Service was split into three departmental roles: the detective element, the preventative side, and the administrative. The detective branch of the Security Service used amongst other things, postal interception. Much like the trend seen in general across the Security Service, their staff numbers grew rapidly as the war progressed. For example, in December 1914, the postal and cable staff of the service numbered some 170 people. By December 1915 this had grown to number 1,453.[21] This demonstrates the extent of the government's fear of German espionage.

Suspects accused of espionage, evidence against whom had been gathered through postal surveillance, were added to a government blacklist. By the war's end some 13,500 people had been added to the blacklist.[22]

The Preventative branch of the Security Service similarly expanded its range of duties. From 1915 it devised many new counter-espionage schemes including: the internment of alien enemies or dangerous persons and their subsequent removal, the creation of prohibited military areas each strictly controlled, which required the creation of offices to issue permits to all those visiting or living there, as well as to

---

[21]'Historical Sketch', 1921, PRO, WO, 32/10776, p20

[22]Kell Papers (Frost), lecture by Kell headed 'Scottish Chief Constables', 26 February 1925, p24

anyone seeking to travel abroad.[23] This expansion of duties further highlights the severity of the perceived threat of espionage felt by the government. The government was prepared from the earliest days of the conflict to severely curtail the personal liberties of the British public and vastly to increase the powers of the secret services.

The underlying pathology of fear can also be seen in another expansion of the preventative branch of the Security Service, when the government gave it the powers to oversee a new Military Port Control Service which was formed in 1915.[24] This sector, according to Vernon Kell, the then head of the Security Service, 'became the deciding factor on who should leave and enter the country'[25].

There is much evidence to suggest that the extensive expansion of the counter-espionage measures taken since the start of the war, in time had, in fact, been hugely successful by 1916. A report by Major Anderson in 1919 claimed that by 1916 it had become exceptionally hard for German agents to operate successful spy networks within Britain. The telegraph interception technology used by the Security Service had improved since 1914. Any messages via telegraph simply became too dangerous to use, making successful espionage and communication extremely difficult.[26] Due to this

---

[23]Kell Papers (Frost), lecture on 'Security Intelligence Work' by Holt Wilson, June 1939, p11

[24]Historical Sketch, 1921, PRO, WO 32/10776, p12

[25]Kell Papers (Frost), lecture on 'Security Intelligence Work' by Holt Wilson, June 1939, p11

[26]Report by Maj Anderson, 28 June 1919, PRO, DEFE 1/30, p104

decreasing threat of espionage, the Security Service turned its attention towards countersubversion rather than counterespionage. The fear was not the threat of military secrets leaking, but rather that German agents were stirring up the industrial disputes to undermine the war effort.[27] The subsequent report on the Secret Service by Major Anderson and the Service's change of tactics in the latter half of the war, suggests that the government's fear of espionage had begun to subside from 1916 onwards.

Day-to-day was affected by counter-espionage measures. Anyone reflecting on the state of individual freedom in early 1914 would have been shocked at the erosion of civil liberties and rights of the individual, by 1916 and none more so than the civilians living in the east of England.

---

[27] https://www.mi5.gov.uk/mi5-in-world-war-i

These Regulations contain PROHIBITIONS AGAINST:—

1. The collection, recording or publication of, or the attempt to elicit, information with respect to Naval or Military matters, or any other information which might be useful to the enemy.
2. The photographing or other representation of any Naval or Military work and the possession in the vicinity of such work, without lawful authority, of apparatus suitable for use in making such representation.
3. Interfering without lawful authority with telegraphic or telephonic apparatus or the possession of apparatus for tapping wireless messages.
4. The keeping, bringing into the United Kingdom, carrying or liberating, of carrier or homing pigeons.
5. The possession of wireless telegraphic apparatus, without the written permission of the Postmaster-General, and the selling of such apparatus to anyone who has not obtained such permission.
6. The conveyance, by hand or otherwise (as distinct from by post), of communications to or from the United Kingdom, originating with, or intended for, an enemy or anyone acting on his behalf.
7. Signalling, and the possession of search lights, semaphores and other signalling apparatus.
8. Displaying, without the permission of the Naval or Military Authority, lights, fireworks or fires, in such a manner as could serve as a signal.
9. The publication of false reports or statements, or of reports or statements likely to cause disaffection, or to prejudice the successful conduct of the war, or to prejudice recruiting or discipline.
10. Trespassing on railways, and loitering near tunnels, bridges, &c., or in any forbidden place.
11. Injuring railways, tunnels, bridges, etc.
12. Approaching within specified distance of camps or defence works.
13. The importation into the United Kingdom of firearms, military arms, ammunition and explosives, without the permit of the competent Authority.
14. Endangering the safety of any member of His Majesty's Forces on duty by the discharge of firearms or otherwise.
15. The possession of firearms and ammunition (except for sporting purposes), or of explosives or highly inflammable liquids in excess of requirements near railways, docks, and harbours, or other places where such possession is prohibited.
16. Supplying intoxicants to members of His Majesty's Forces when on sentry or other duty, or (with intent to make them drunk or incapable) when not on duty.
17. The unauthorised use of official uniforms, and the supply of naval and military uniforms to unauthorised persons.
18. The attempt to cause mutiny, sedition, or disaffection.
19. The obstruction of, or withholding information from, officers or other persons carrying out orders of competent Naval or Military Authorities.
20. The falsification of reports with intent to mislead officers on duty.
21. Forgery or personation of passes and permits.
22. The possession of false passports, and, in the case of enemies, the passing under assumed names.
23. Non-compliance with any order issued by the competent Naval or Military Authority.
24. The aiding or abetting of any prohibited act.
25. The non-disclosure of any contravention of the Regulations.

The Defence of the Realm Act first passed into UK law on the 8 August 1914, following the outbreak of war, with incredible speed and without any debate in Parliament. The Act was intended to aid in the government's home defence policies and counter-espionage measures by gaining control of communications, the nation's ports and subject civilians to the rule of military. The act was revised on multiple occasions throughout the war's duration enabling the government to utilize never before seen powers and subjecting civilians to countless new regulations. These regulations were relayed to the public in many ways such as through posters such as this.

The Defence of the Realm Regulations also confer upon the competent Naval or Military Authority the following, amongst other powers:—

1. To take possession of any land or buildings; to destroy any property or do any other act interfering with private rights of property.
2. To have access to any land or buildings.
3. To use land for the training of troops.
4. To stop or divert roads.
5. To require the removal of vehicles, live stock, foodstuffs, fuel or tools from a specified area.
6. To require the removal of inhabitants from specified areas.
7. To require licensed premises to be closed.
8. To direct that all lights visible from the outside of any house shall be extinguished or obscured within specified hours.
9. To require inhabitants to remain indoors between specified hours.
10. To order the removal of suspected persons and to prescribe the areas within which they may reside.
11. To require a census of specified goods.
12. To require the preparation by the person in control of a scheme for destruction of harbour works, gas or electric light or power works, etc.
13. To prohibit persons from having in their possession telegraphic, telephonic or other apparatus for sending or receiving messages.
14. To prevent the embarkation of persons suspected of communicating with the enemy.
15. To require or procure the removal of flagstaffs or other apparatus for signalling.
16. To prevent persons approaching within a specified distance of a camp or work of defence.
17. To prohibit the manufacture and sale of arms, ammunition and explosives.
18. To search ships arriving from abroad for arms, ammunition and explosives.
19. To control the navigation and pilotage of ships.
20. To enter and search buildings, ships, land, vehicles, and other premises at any time, and to seize and destroy things found therein kept or in use in contravention of the Regulations.
21. To stop and search vehicles.
22. To require persons to furnish information.
23. To require the production of any letters or other written messages in the possession of persons landing or embarking in the United Kingdom, and to search any such person or any baggage for such letters or messages, and to examine any letters or messages found on such search.
24. To arrest without warrant persons suspected of acting prejudicially to the safety of the Realm.
25. To require the production of permits.

SEVERE PENALTIES ARE PRESCRIBED FOR CONTRAVENTION OF THE DEFENCE OF THE REALM REGULATIONS.

Poster from 1915 detailing regulations of the Aliens Restriction Act 1914.

The Aliens Restriction Act first passed in 1914 gave the government sweeping powers to control the movements of Germans living in the United Kingdom in order to limit the threats posed by German espionage.

Post-war poster urging the population to be wary of German civilians living in Britain. Posters such as this are consistent with views held by the British public and authorities throughout the war.

City of London Police poster on the Aliens Restriction Act 1914 regulations.

This poster issued by the City of London Police notified the public that any member of the public of German citizenship was subject to a curfew at their designated registered address between the hours of 9pm and 5am in which the failure to comply would result in the arrest of those breaching said rules. Regulations such as these demonstrate the effect governmental counter-espionage measures had on those who lived in the east of England and highlight how Germans living in Britain often faced dragonian regulations.

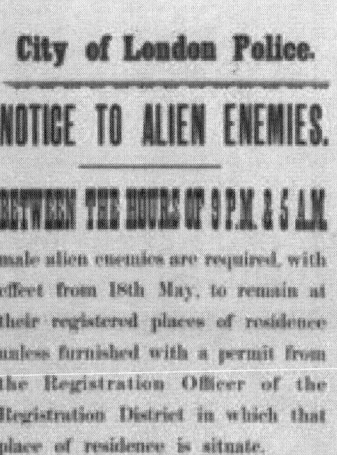

5

PARANOIA AND HYSTERIA

Public Reactions to the Fear of German Invasion Attempts on the East of England

THERE WAS A GENERAL AND GROWING worry that the stalemate on the western front would provide the opportunity for Germany to launch an invasion in the east of England. The novelist, Arnold Bennett, then living in Thorp-le-Soken in Essex, captured the mood in the east of England, noting on 10 August 1914 that 'At the back of the mind of everyone is a demi-semi fear lest the Germans should after all by some coup, contrive an invasion'.[1] Bennett said that within a matter of weeks following the outbreak of war his household had begun to discuss their plans should the German forces land in England. Similarly, Stanley Bird, who lived in Colchester, adamantly maintained that he knew an attempted invasion by German forces upon the eastern coast to be a real possibility following the outbreak of war between

---

[1] A. Bennett writing on 10 August 1914, in, Pennell, 'The Germans have Landed', p102

the two nations.² These two accounts from the locality help indicate the vivid fears of invasion at the outbreak of the war. Essex historian, Ken Porter, supports the accounts of Bennett and Bird, noting that 'After the initial euphoria and celebrations following the declaration of war, reality slowly began to sink in' where soon the realities of a major European conflict and the 'fear of invasion began to occupy people's minds'³

Fears of an attempted German invasion of the east coast of England in 1914 were fuelled mainly by the brutal and shocking German invasion of Belgium in August 1914. The invasion confirmed pre-war British prejudices about German military aggression. These anxieties were to be found in their most concentrated form in the eastern counties. There, people had long been aware of their military vulnerability.

Both national and local newspaper articles helped to enlarge these concerns. Accounts of the activities of German soldiers during the invasion of Belgium were exaggerated for propaganda purposes. On 25 August 1914 the *Chelmsford Chronicle* published an article which compared the invasion of Belgium by German forces to that of a biblical invasion and suggested that the fight Britain and her allies now found themselves in was a battle between the forces of good and evil.⁴ British soldiers serving on the front lines in Belgium and France in the early months of the war also reported

---

²The Imperial War Museum Sound Archives, 7375: Reel 1

³K. Porter, 'Clacton on Sea', p49

⁴'How History Repeats Itself', *Chelmsford Chronicle*, 25 September 1914, p2

many atrocities committed by the invading Germans. One such account from a British soldier detailed how German forces shelled a hospital as well as killing the wounded whilst describing how they are 'cruel and have no pity'.[5] Similarly, another account by a British soldier told of how a Belgian toddler was pinned to a wall by a German's sword which he described as simply a moderate act of German barbarism.[6]

William Le Queux, the famous pre-war invasion author, wrote that the Germans were 'one vast army of Jack-the-Rippers'[7] and detailed in graphic accounts the savagery of the German army. Public imaginings of the German army often hearkened to Ripper-like activities where there were numerous tales of sadistic mutilations of nurses' breasts by German soldiers as well as the rape of Belgian women on a mass scale. These sickening and grim reports, which no doubt had caused intense panic in the nervous public of the east of England, were reinforced by government rhetoric. The Prime Minister himself, Herbert Asquith, in a speech in Cardiff in October 1914, described the German army as 'hordes who leave behind them at every stage of their progress a dismal trail of savagery, of devastation, of desecration worthy of the blackest annals in the history of barbarism'.[8] The Prime

---

[5] 'German Barbarities', *Cambridge Independent Press*, 11 September 1914, p6

[6] 'Child Pinned with a Sword', *Suffolk and Essex Free Press*, 9 December 1914, p7

[7] Nicoletta Gullace, *The Blood of Our Sons: Men, Women, and the Renegotiation of British Citizenship During the Great War* (Palgrave Macmillan, 2002)

Minister's referral to the likes of 'hordes' and 'barbarism' was no doubt perhaps an unsubtle comparison of the German army to the barbarian tribes which had stormed through Europe during the fall of the Roman Empire and had ushered in the so-called Dark Ages and the end of European civilisation. These words would have stirred tensions and fears about a possible invasion and its consequences. The German soldier represented destruction and the end of British civilisation.

Many reports of German savagery and barbarism during the invasion of Belgium were greatly exaggerated by the government and the press for propaganda purposes. These reports fed the public mood of anxiety and jingoism. The reality of what was called the 'rape of Belgium' was in fact stark. It is estimated that the invasion of Belgium and the subsequent occupation of the German forces led to the deaths of approximately 23,700 Belgian civilians either through combat, expulsion, imprisonment, or execution. In comparison it is estimated that 26,386 Belgian soldiers were killed during this period. This figure indicates the disproportionate civilian losses and the savage reality of life for those caught up in modern warfare. Aside from the immense death toll amongst Belgian civilians, many more remained injured and mutilated. Nearly 34,000 civilians sustained permanent or temporary injuries as a result of the invasion.[9] Furthermore, on 25 August, there was

---

[8]Various authors, *Great Speeches of the War* (London: Hazell, Watson & Viney Ltd, 1915), p1

[9]'Annuaire statistique de la Belgique et du Congo Belge, 1915-1919', Bruxelles, 1922, p100

international outcry following the sack of Leuven, when German forces ransacked the historic town. Three hundred civilians were killed in the rampage with a further 10,000 being forced to flee their homes. Shockingly, in their rampage, German troops deliberately torched the library of the university, resulting in the loss of thousands of medieval manuscripts. Arson would form a common feature of the invasion of Belgium, where in Leuven alone some 2,000 buildings were destroyed.

The invasion of Belgium and the subsequent frenzy of alarmist press reports that followed undoubtedly increased dread and paranoia in the east of England of an imminent invasion by German forces. These events legitimised pre-war fears of invasion. A Chelmsford minister noted in the *Essex Newsman* in September 1914 that 'we in Essex are by no means free of the danger of invasion'.[10] The legacy of the invasion of Belgium in the public consciousness can also be seen in members of local organisations. The minutes of Latchingford Parish Council, for example, noted in December 1914 that its members had to face:

> a far more serious and urgent matter and that was what were they to do in the event of an invasion by a hostile foe, they all know what had happened in Belgium and the northern part of France, and the same thing or even worse would happen in England, if the enemy could ever effect a landing. It therefore behoves every able-bodied person to do all that they possibly could for the safety of the women, children and infirm.[11]

---

[10] 'Chelmsford Minister and the Kaiser', *Essex Newsman*, 26 September 1914, p2

[11] Minutes of the Latchingford Parish Council, 10 December 1914, in Pennel, 'The Germans Have Landed', p109

These minutes explicitly demonstrate how the subject of invasion was always of the highest priority for the local authorities. Furthermore, the Council's call to the local people further highlights that this was a threat taken very seriously indeed and was a threat so dire and desperate that everyone must play their part.

The frenzy of press reports, government propaganda, as well as the tales of horror brought back to the east of England by returning British soldiers and the masses of Belgian refugees seeking safety in England, all culminated to form an atmosphere of seething paranoia and hysteria within the populations of the east coast. In the months following the invasion of Belgium there were numerous reports of false alarms: the *Essex Standard*, for one, detailed how a panic had arisen after reports of gunshots, with locals believing they were under attack from German aircraft. In fact, a local sentry had simply shot at a cat.

In hindsight it is easy to judge these local panics as products of war psychosis. Actual events must have certainly given those living in the east of England a sense that invasion could be just around the corner. Between 19 October and 30 November 1914 in southern Belgium, the first battle of Ypres was raging between the Allied forces and the German army. The battle was so intense that it nearly resulted in the destruction of the British Expeditionary Force. The prospects of an invasion of Britain seemed all the nearer.

Aside from the very real sense of foreboding in eastern England brought about by the lightning invasion of neutral Belgium, there were other events closer to home which certainly increased the public's sense that an attack was imminent. As we saw earlier there were active concerns in the government and military authorities that the prevailing stalemate might encourage Germany to attempt to launch an invasion. The theory was that, with the British, French, and Belgian forces bogged down in the western theatre, the German forces could adopt solely defensive measures to hold back the Allied armies. This would release men and material to mount an invasion upon Britain. If successful, the invasion would almost inevitably knock Britain out of the war.

But was this scenario based on any military reality? During 'the race for the sea', in late 1914, in which the Allied and German armies raced to control the vital channel ports of France, Germany was unable to capture the major French ports of Calais, Boulogne or Dunkirk. These failures were a significant blow for German chances of a successful invasion. Germany was denied a naval foothold in the English Channel which would have been essential to any invasion of southern England. Some believed failure to seize the ports effectively destroyed any real chance of invasion. However, German forces still controlled the major Belgian ports of Ostend and Zeebrugge, enabling the German Imperial Navy access to the southern waters of the North Sea. While chances of an invasion of southern counties seemed to have been snuffed out, there was still a threat to the eastern counties. Germany's only possible chance of any successful invasion would entail using captured Belgian ports for landings along the coastline of East Anglia, which offered advancing troops a close proximity to London.

Events would exacerbate these fears even further. On the morning of 3 November 1914, the usually peaceful tranquillity of the Norfolk coastal town of Great Yarmouth was shattered by the explosions of German shells landing on the local beach. Fortunately for the town's residents the barrage proved to be short and ineffective with the only damage being limited to the beach. The German battlecruisers that undertook the raid: the SMS Seydlitz, SMS Von der Taan, SMS Moltke, the light cruisers: SMS Gaudenz, SMS Kolberg, SMS Straslund, and the armoured cruiser SMS Blucher, were intercepted and fired upon by HMS Halycon, HMS Lively, and HMS Success, confusing the German attack and rendering it far less accurate.

In strictly military terms, the raid proved a near outright failure. Not only had the German Navy failed to cause any extensive damage to Great Yarmouth but in the process had lost the armoured cruiser SMS Yorck as it left its home port to aid the raiding ships.

Despite this loss, there were some positives for the German Navy as a result of the attack. It had managed to enter British waters with ease and had led the British to lose one submarine and three fishing trawlers. The raid proved to be successful psychologically, undermining people's confidence in the invincibility of the Royal Navy. The fact the war had been suddenly brought so close to their shores, proved a severe shock for many residents. Initially it was believed that the explosions could not possibly be a result of a German attack. The short bombardment resulted in a 'hurried flight' of people fleeing the town, many of them still in their night clothes. As the raid continued rumours began to circulate around the Norfolk coast where the distant rumble of the guns could be heard 'spreading alarm everywhere'.[12] Given that a belief already existed that an invasion might happen at any time people in Great Yarmouth and the surrounding areas would, no doubt, have thought this raid might be a prelude to an invasion. Even for those who did not believe the much-feared invasion was on its way, the attack would have brought home to those living on the east coast the grim reality that even if an invasion was not coming, they were by no means safe. The shelling of Great Yarmouth, alongside the more brutal, deadly and successful raids upon the northeastern ports of Scarborough, Hartlepool and Whitby on 16 December 1914, meant that threat of invasion was now coupled with the threat of indiscriminate bombardments.

While local fears were understandable, the naval reality, however, was somewhat different. The German navy wasn't interested in preparing for an invasion or even launching a form of psychological warfare on those living in Britain's eastern counties.

In the North Sea the Royal Navy, well aware of its superiority over the German fleet, kept their warships grouped together in order to maintain this advantage in any sea battle. Possibly as a counter to this, the attack on Great Yarmouth can also be seen as part of a German plan to lure smaller fleets of British ships to the town's rescue, giving the German Navy greater opportunities to inflict damage on British vessels.

---

[12]<https://www.edp24.co.uk/features/great-yarmouth-s-lucky-escape-and-the-failed-bombardment-1-3830399> [accessed 26 August 2020]

By 1915, articles in local newspapers detailing the topic of invasion had decreased slightly in the east of England, going from 416 in 1914 down to 378 by 1915. However, this reduction was not dramatic enough to suggest with any conviction that anxiety within the local population had decreased.[13] By 1915, the stalemate on the western front that had existed since the winter of 1914, was not guaranteed to last. Many feared that when the weather turned milder the German army could break out past the Allied lines and make another attempt to capture the French channel ports, thus increasing the risk of an attempted invasion of Britain. For example, a speaker at an army recruitment meeting in Burston, Norfolk, stated that invasion would prove to be easy if the Germans were able to capture the remainder of the Belgian coast and the French channel ports, clearly suggesting that stalemate in the eyes of the military and public of East Anglia had by no means written off the possibility of invasion.[14] This fear is reinforced by the *Cambridge Independent Press* which noted on 30 April 1915 that 'there was still a danger of invasion'.[15] These examples highlight that worries about an invasion of the east of England certainly persisted throughout the first two years of the war. Compared to the broader national situation, there is a clear difference in the fear and threats of invasion between those

---

[13]BNA<https://www.britishnewspaperarchive.co.uk/search> [accessed 12 April 2019]

[14]'Burston Recruitment Meeting', *Diss Express*, 26 February 1916, p4

[15]*Cambridge Independent Press*, 30 April 1915, p6

living in the east of England and those living in other areas of Britain. For example, one article in a regional Norfolk paper, *Diss Express*, noted in November 1915 that 'Worcestershire and Suffolk were about as differently constituted with regard to the war as two counties could be'. Suffolk with its long wide beaches was perceived by most to be a dangerous area liable to the risk of invasion. Worcestershire, on the other hand, situated far inland to the west, was in no pressing danger of invasion. The article further notes the large responsibility of the local population in the county due to threat of invasion.[16] Whilst the fear of invasion in 1915 remained as strong as in 1914 amongst the people of eastern England, there is also some evidence to suggest that the fears were easing somewhat. For example, the *Bedfordshire Times and Independent* reported that following the outbreak of hostilities in 1914 there had been many inquiries from members of the public in regards to what action should be undertaken in the event of an invasion, but recently these enquiries had decreased.[17] Alternatively, this is just as likely a product of the success of the efforts made by the authorities to relay crucial information to the public, rather than a reduced fear of invasion in itself.

By the close of 1916 two years had passed since the outbreak of war and the German invasions of Belgium and north-eastern France. The western front since the winter of 1914 had become a war of stalemate and attrition. By the

---

[16]'East Suffolk County Council', *Diss Express*, 19 November 1915, p5

[17]'In Case of Invasion', *Bedfordshire Times and Independent*, 12 March 1915, p5

summer of 1916 the European powers, both on the western front and the eastern front, were engulfed in three of the largest and most brutal battles of the war.

On the western front, in what was to become the longest and bloodiest battle of the war, the French and German armies were engaged in a brutally relentless back and forth battle to capture the highly defendable banks of the river Meuse just east of the medieval town of Verdun. The German army planned to force the collapse of the French army through attrition, by capturing the strategic Meuse heights, which they believed would compel the French to attempt to recapture this position and thus suffer casualties at a staggering rate. In a statement that would come to define the Battle of Verdun, the German Chief of Staff, Eric Von Falkenhayn, declared that 'the forces of France will bleed to death'. Meanwhile, to the north of Verdun, the Germans found themselves defending an allied attack of epic proportions near the river Somme. Between 1 July and 18 November 1916, British and French troops aimed to break through the German lines to force a decisive victory. Despite some successes the British and French ultimately failed to conclusively break the German lines and became, like Verdun, one of the most brutal and costliest battles of the war. On the eastern front, the German, Austro-Hungarian, and Ottoman forces, after years of success, found themselves engulfed in a brutal defensive war against an enormous advancing Russian army. Between 4 June and 10 August 1916, in what was to be called the Brusilov Offensive, the forces of the Russian Empire inflicted severe damage to the Triple Alliance. The offensive, which became Russia's greatest of the war, caused the Austrian army to be so exhausted in military terms that it would not be able to recover for the rest of the war. The Habsburg Empire was now on the verge of collapse, forced to rely more and more upon Berlin. As the historian, Graydon Tunstall, has argued the Brusilov Offensive was the greatest victory of the First World War for the Triple Entente, provoking, as noted above, an ever-deepening sense of crisis for Austro-Hungarians.[18] Throughout 1916, the German army, as a result, were forced to commit millions of men and military materials to the western and eastern fronts, suffering a staggering 963,501 casualties.[19] With German troops and war materials stretched over multiple fronts and suffering horrendous casualties it is no surprise that the chances of a German invasion had, in the minds of most, become far slimmer.

In the light of the gargantuan battles raging between the warring powers on the European continent throughout 1916, there is further evidence that the fear of invasion had decreased in the east of England since the previous year. Articles regarding invasion in the local newspapers had fallen from 378 in 1915 to 267, emphasising a significant decrease from 1914 and 1915.[20] However, whilst articles detailing the threat of invasion had fallen in number, it is worth noting

---

[18]Graydon A. Tunstall, 'Austria-Hungary and the Brusilov Offensive of 1916' (2008), *The Historian* 70 (1): 30-53 [p52]. doi: 10.1111/j.1540-6563.2008.00202.x

[19]Robert Weldon Whalen, *Bitter Wounds: German Victims of the Great War*, Ithaca 1984, pp39-40

[20]BNA <https://www.britishnewspaperarchive.co.uk/search/results> [accessed 12 April 2019]

that the volunteer forces in Essex had increased in size following a decline, rising from 2,000 volunteers to 5,000 by late 1916, indicating that there were still genuine invasion fears in eastern England.[21] Whilst the strength of the Volunteer Training Corps had, on a national scale, decreased as the Great War went on, the numbers of volunteers in Essex grew. The national experience differed from that of the east of England. It might also reflect the broader growth in the prominence of the home front, where civilians increasingly found their lives affected by the brutality and totality of the war. In this atmosphere, many civilians across Britain believed, more and more, that they must play their part in the war effort, for example, women going to work to replace those at the front.

An article titled 'The Danger of Invasion' in the *Chelmsford Chronicle* in 1916, reported a meeting held locally to discuss London's defences. The article stated that the meeting drew in a large crowd. Interest in home defence had not abated. The speaker stated however that there existed a general belief in government that an invasion by Germany was no longer possible due to the Royal Navy's 'victory' over the Imperial Navy at the Battle of Jutland between 31 May and 1 June 1916. The German navy had failed to destroy significant elements of the British fleet. In contrast to the government view the speaker stated that he believed Germany might attempt an invasion after rebuilding its fleet.[22] With hindsight, we now know that the Battle of Jutland seriously

---

[21]'Essex Volunteer Force', *Chelmsford Chronicle*, 13 October 1916, p5

[22]'The Danger of Invasion', *Chelmsford Chronicle*, 23 June 1916, p5

damaged Germany's capability to carry out any invasion plan. Germany kept the bulk of its fleet out of British waters. Germany then focused its main attention to unrestricted submarine warfare in the Atlantic. The people living in the east of England believed that the war could have still gone in any direction: invasion was still a possibility.

From 1917 onwards, fears of any German invasion seem to have lessened in eastern England, with local newspaper articles detailing invasion decreasing to 203, a significant drop from the numbers in 1916, and further decreasing in 1918, falling to 146 articles.[23]

From 1916 onwards, it becomes apparent that the worries of those living in the east of England were moving away from the threat of invasion towards new and more legitimate threats. One such new worry was German naval attacks on ports along the eastern coast. Raids on British coastal towns had opened the people of eastern England up to the reality of indiscriminate, random attack. The reality of seemingly random attacks on coastal towns was reinforced not from the sea, but from the air. Aerial attacks had begun, most notably from Zeppelin airships.

The Zeppelin, a form of rigid airship made by Count Ferdinand von Zeppelin, was relatively new technology when war broke out. The Zeppelin would become one of the most easily identifiable symbols of the First World War, and in Britain would form one of the enduring images of the home front experience. Since the 1890s, von Zeppelin had tried

---

[23]BNA <https://www.britishnewspaperarchive.co.uk/search/results> [accessed 12 April 2019]

and failed many times to prove the importance of his new airship to the German military. After years of failures, he managed to convince them. The first proposals to bomb Britain had been made by Paul Behncke, the then Deputy Chief of the German Naval staff in August 1914, and was, importantly, supported by Admiral von Tirpitz, the Chief of the German Naval staff. Kaiser Wilhelm II approved military plans to attack Britain through the use of Zeppelins in January 1915, but strictly forbade attacks on London, fearing his relatives in the British Royal family might be harmed. Following Wilhelm's approval, the first successful raid upon England was carried out on the night of 19 and 20 January 1915. Two Zeppelins crossed the North Sea to target British ports on Humberside. However, strong January winds deterred them from reaching their targets. As the Zeppelins returned home the crew dropped their bombs on the East Anglian towns of Sherringham, Kings Lynn, Great Yarmouth, and other local villages. The attack resulted in four deaths, sixteen injured civilians and £195,000 worth of damage. This sudden and surprising attack from the air ushered in a new era of modern warfare. The public in the east of England had begrudgingly accepted that their status as civilians no longer secured them immunity from the horrors of war. No civilians had expected or anticipated attacks from the air. The attack on the East Anglian towns further prompted alarmist reports that German spies had guided the Zeppelins.

In the spring of 1915 the Germans launched a new aerial offensive against Britain using the new, modified p-class Zeppelin. On the night of 29 to 30 April, LZ38, piloted by

Erich Linnarz, conducted the first of these raids when his crew bombed the Suffolk port town of Ipswich. This was followed by two other raids on the east of England when the same Zeppelin attacked the Essex coastal town of Southend on the night of 19 to 20 May and the night of 26 to 27 May. It also conducted raids on the ports of Dover and Ramsgate on 16 to 17 May. The Zeppelin, for the most part, in 1915 was able to bomb its targets with impunity from aerial interception, with its only real adversaries being the weather or the anti-aircraft guns surrounding the capital. In all these raids the Royal Naval Air Service (the precursor to the Royal Air Force) had attempted to intercept them with aeroplanes, which proved to be technologically inferior to the Zeppelins and could neither climb quicker than, nor reach the same altitude as, the Zeppelins. In all four raids undertaken by the airship LZ38 six people were killed and a further six were injured. In the light of the type of bombings humanity would witness as the century progressed, these figures seem tame and miniscule. However, we cannot dismiss the psychological trauma this would inflict upon those living in the east of England who could now at any time anticipate attack from the air without the possibility of interception. Raids such as these upon the east of England were to continue throughout 1915, such as L10's raid on the Essex port of Harwich, or on 24 April 1916, Norwich, Harwich, and Ipswich, bombed as part of simultaneous naval bombardment of Great Yarmouth and Lowestoft.

In mid-1915 the Kaiser finally relented to the wishes of his military staff, and on 30 May authorised the first Zeppelin raid on London. These raids on the capital would occur multiple times between 1915 and 1916, the vast majority of which passed over Essex and other counties in the east of England on their way to targets in London. They used the River Thames or the Great Eastern Railway as a guide.

Whilst the Zeppelin was unmatched in the air, its vulnerability to anti-aircraft fire had great repercussions for people living in Essex. Zeppelin crews, unable to penetrate London's defences, often dropped their bombs over the eastern counties as they returned to their bases. On the night of 23 September 1916, in what was the single largest raid of the war so far, twelve Zeppelins crossed the channel to bomb targets in the Midlands, the Northeast, and London. Two of the Zeppelins taking part in the raid, the L32 and L31, bombed parts of London before both crashing in Essex. The L31 had been hit by anti-aircraft fire and, whilst not immediately crashing, was forced to make a landing in Little Wigborough in Essex, narrowly missing some cottages. L32, on its return from London, was intercepted and shot down by 2nd Lieutenant Frederick Sowery, its flaming wreckage landing in Great Burstead, Essex. The image of these two vast Zeppelins crashing over the Essex skyline caused a sensation across the county. Rose Luard, who lived near Little Wigborough, described how after hearing the distant sound of bombs and gunfire which made their windows 'rattle', her family rushed to the window to watch the Zeppelin crashing to the ground, and when inspecting the wreckage described it as a 'vast monster',[24] a metaphor which suggests the overarching fear it represented to civilians. In the days

---

[24]Transcript of Rose Luard's letter describing the landing of Zeppelin L31 in Little Wigborough, 24 September 1916 (D/DLu 76)

following the raid the crash sites at Great Burstead and Little Wigborough were engulfed with people as crowds arrived en masse to witness the vast burnt-out wrecks of the infamous Zeppelins. At the crash site in Great Burstead, for instance, it was reported that crowds even arrived from as far away as London. In Little Wigborough, things got even more out of hand as onlookers flocked to the wreckage of the airship, with police sergeant McDiamid reporting the 'immense' crowds of tourists and, strangely, the arrival of 'six British aeroplanes and a British airship' that had come along to see the wreckage.[25]

In local newspapers there are many articles which demonstrate a widespread fear of Zeppelin attack in eastern counties. Many of these articles, including the opinions and thoughts of local people at this time, contribute to the idea that fears of German land invasions upon the east of England had been temporarily replaced by the fear of Zeppelin raids. The *Essex Newsman*, for example, reporting in May 1915, ran the headline of 'Another Air Raid at Southend' and reported that the German airmen piloting the airship had dropped notes from the sky onto the Essex ground stating that more and ever greater raids upon the east of England were imminent.[26] This article not only suggests a deep-rooted fear of Zeppelin raids in the region as early as the spring of 1915, but also contributes to our understanding of how panic of this sort spread throughout the area. The menacing notes dropped from the sky, alongside the actual Zeppelin raids

---

[25]http://www.essexrecordofficeblog.co.uk/zeppelins-over-essex/

[26]'Another Air Raid at Southend', *Essex Newsman*, 29 May 1915, p3

ever increasing in their size, strength, and frequency, formed part of a number of factors which convinced the people living in counties such as Essex that Zeppelin raids were the major and more immediate threat to safety. Leading on from this, the *Essex Newsman* again provides evidence that the fear of Zeppelin raids may have temporarily overtaken that of invasion.[27] When a local meeting in Essex was discussing the matter of civilian armament, a pacifist declared he was unsure whether he could kill another person, even if the person in question was a German airman that had landed in his area. This to me demonstrates how, subconsciously, the fear of invasion had been somewhat overtaken as the most pressing threat to eastern England. In the early stages of the war, people had often used the scenario of an invading German soldier when discussing whether or not one could kill for their country. This image was replaced with the invading German airman. Subtle details such as these demonstrate the conscious and subconscious anxieties of those living close to the eastern coast. Fear of Zeppelin raids over the skies of the east of England can also be shown in the *Essex Newsman*, where Essex residents expressed their fears that undimmed lights would guide Zeppelins to towns such as Billericay.[28] Finally, in terms of the articles from the local newspapers, far more stories ran on the topic of Zeppelins than on the subject of invasion. For example, between 1914 and 1918, there were 1,410 articles detailing the topic of invasion, compared to 2,382 articles concerning Zeppelins. In 1916

---

[27] '1,000 Appeals', *Essex Newsman*, 15 April 1915, p4

[28] 'Police Courts', *Essex Newsman*, 22 January 1916, p3

alone, there were 267 articles on invasion and 1,018 on Zeppelins – a huge difference, suggesting that the Zeppelin was perceived as the greater threat.

By late 1916, however, major improvements in the efficiency and range of anti-aircraft artillery, as well as considerable improvements in the capabilities of aerial interception aircraft, limited the effectiveness of Zeppelins, and thus Zeppelin raids decreased. The Zeppelin was then slowly replaced by the far quicker Gotha Bombers which had an overall lower impact on the east of England.

Remember Belgium enlistment poster.

The plight of Belgium was used as a major recruitment tool for the British Army in the early years of the war, where posters such as this were dispersed across the United Kingdom. Posters like this also proved to be a striking visual reminder to the civilians of the east of England of the possible consequences of invasion.

Photograph depicting ruins of the city of Leuven.

During the invasion of Belgium German soldiers sacked the medieval city of Leuven. In doing so over 2,000 buildings were destroyed, 248 residents were killed, and the university library was deliberately torched by German soldiers, resulting in the destruction of thousands of medieval manuscripts.

Painting by Evariste Carpentier depicting the execution of civilians in Blegny, Belgium

Paintings such as this were seen across the world and served to emphasise the allied nations' view of German soldiers as warmongering and blood thirsty.

GERMAN ATROCITIES.

BELGIAN OFFICIAL ACCOUNT OF LOUVAIN.

The Belgian Commission of Inquiry into the violation of the rules governing the rights of people and of the laws and customs of war has issued its fifth report.

It contains a pathetic letter from Mme. Tielemans (widow of the Burgomaster of Aerschot), who gives an account of the circumstances which preceded the execution of her innocent husband and son.

In some rural localities, says the report, whole villages have been wiped out, and the population, without shelter or bread, has fled to the woods. In ditches along the route lie unburied bodies of unfortunate peasants, including women and children. Some corpses have been thrown into wells, contaminating the water.

It is only, says the report, when the German occupation of the country is ended that it will be possible to ascertain, commune by commune, town by town, the full enormity of the German atrocities.

Article on the German atrocities in Belgium, *Diss Express*, 9 October 1914. Articles like this reinforced a fear in the population of the east of England of the fate that could await them in the event of a German invasion.

IN CASE OF INVASION.

MEETING AT SOUTHMINSTER.

A public meeting was held in the Schoolroom, Southminster, on Tuesday evening, under the auspices of the Southminster Emergency Committee. There was a large attendance. Mr. G. Raby, J.P., C.A., presided, and was supported by Messrs. Chas Tarr (chairman of the Parish Council), Primrose McConnell, J. W. Sugden, F Cresswell, and E. S. Foster.

The Chairman read instructions issued by the Government as to what was to be done by the public in the event of an invasion by the enemy. He said there were about fifty wagons at the disposal of the committee, and these could be used to convey the thousand women and children of Southminster to a place of safety. The route to be taken was by the back roads to Althorne, and then on to the first line of defence. The public were to keep to the back roads as much as possible, and leave the main roads for the use of the military authorities. Each person must take sufficient provisions to last at

Article on local preparations in the event of a German invasion, *Chelmsford Chronicle*, 25 December 1914.

'Men of Britain! Will you stand this?', recruitment poster, 1915.

On 16 December 1914 a massive raid by German naval ships occurred on the British coastal towns of Scarborough, Hartlepool and Whitby, resulting in enormous damage and 592 casualties, many of whom were civilians. The raid caused outrage across Britain with posters such as this one being used in recruitment drives for the British Army. This particular poster detailed the destruction of a house in Scarborough, noting that four people in this house had died as a result of the bombardment.

'Remember Scarborough? Enlist now!'
Recruitment poster, Lucy E. Kemp Welch, 1914.

WWI army recruitment poster, Franks Vali.

The Zeppelin raids over London and the east of England shocked the population who were unused to the concept of British civilians being attacked in war.

Photograph depicting the wreckage of the Zeppelin L31, Little Wigborough, Essex, September 1916.

On the night of 23 September 1916 an enormous raid consisting of 12 Zeppelins took place over England. The attack, however, resulted in the downing of two Zeppelins over Essex with the L31 landing in Little Wigborough and the L32 landing in Great Burstead. At both crash sites tourists arrived in huge numbers showing the fascination such aircraft inspired.

Essex Newsman, 5 December 1914.

Newspaper article giving safety advice to civilians.

6

SPY FEVER

Public Reactions to the Fear of German
Espionage in the East of England

HOW PREVALENT AND INTENSE WERE FEARS of the presence of German spies? How were these fears manifested?

Political tensions between Britain and Germany, combined with the popularity of spy and invasion literature, created spy fever in the British public. The historian David French summarised the extent of this fever, stating that the 'myth of the evil and ubiquitous German spy' became 'increasingly virulent in the decade or so before the war'.[1] However, any form of spy fever that existed in the public before the war pales in comparison to the hysterical spy fever that gripped the nation during the war itself, with French noting that by August 1914 'mutual distrust had become mutual hatred'.[2]

In the east of England there was an all-pervasive public fear of espionage, especially in the initial chaos of the early

---

[1] David French, *Spy Fever*, p355

[2] David French, *Spy Fever*, p364

years of the war. This was due to a mixture of government warnings and propaganda regarding the presence of spies, sensationalist press reports, and widespread pre-existing and new fears such as air raids.

In the immediate aftermath of the outbreak of war, there was a determined attack against Germans living in Britain. Newspapers called for companies to dismiss any German employee. The press wanted Germans barred from clubs and societies. Given the pervasive fears concerning invasion existed in the decades prior to 1914, as well as the immense popularity of spy literature, meant that this was unsurprising. Author William Le Queux had warned the people that there was a hidden army of German spies living at all levels of society. These spies, from the highest offices in the land to waiters and shopkeepers, would undertake vital reconnaissance work on targets of interest to the German High Command. Additionally, they were ready to carry out the sabotage of the nation's infrastructure in the event of a German landing. Such notions had become deeply rooted. In September 1914, for example, only one month after the declaration of war, the police in London had 'received nearly 9,000 reports from the public of suspicious Germans ... almost without exception they were found to be groundless'.[3] This statistic demonstrates the gulf between reality and public perceptions of the dangers posed by supposed spies and fifth columnists.

Nowhere was that gulf bigger than in the east of England. At that time this region comprised many rural isolated

---

[3]David French, *Spy Fever*, p365

communities traditionally suspicious of outsiders. Yet the fears of those living in Britain's eastern counties were not wholly irrational. The region's potential vulnerability and high military importance, as well as pre-war spy literature, added credibility to the idea of thousands of spies living along the east coast.

Local newspapers of the time showed how widespread anxiety was about German spies and sympathisers. For example, by the end of 1914 there had been about 237 articles published in the local press referring to the topic of spies[4] with a further 63 on the topic of espionage.[5] One article in the *Suffolk and Essex Free Press* detailed the dangers of spies in the area and their plots. One story described how a barmaid overheard German operatives discussing, in German, espionage plans involving the use of dynamite. Unbeknownst to the alleged spies, the barmaid understood German and had the pair arrested.

The truth of the story is certainly debatable. It could have been just a rumour that gained credibility, or the story could have been exaggerated and twisted, either by the barmaid or the newspaper itself.[6] The repercussions of this hothouse atmosphere of paranoia and suspicion were felt the hardest by German immigrants or those of German extraction. On 8 August 1914, there was a brief spy scare in the Essex town

---

[4]BNA <https://www.britishnewspaperarchive.co.uk/search/results> [accessed 23 April 2019]

[5]BNA <https://www.britishnewspaperarchive.co.uk/search/results> [accessed 14 April 2019]

[6]'German Spy Danger', *Suffolk and Essex Free Press*, 9 September 1914, p6

of Braintree where a man described as having 'Germanic features' was arrested in a local barbershop after a suspicious barber reported him to the police. The *Essex Newsman* which published the story, however, admitted it was highly unlikely that he was a spy.[7] Those of German background or citizenship were not the only victims of public paranoia in the east of England. Paranoia in the small rural and isolated villages in the eastern counties meant that an Ordnance Survey mapper, whilst surveying the local area, was treated with hostility and suspicion. It was believed that he was a German spy on reconnaissance duty. He then required military protection during future trips.[8]

Ultimately fear of espionage can be seen by the intense public speculation and deep interest shown in cases of alleged spies. The *Yarmouth Independent* in September 1914 reported the 'tremendous' excitement in a village when a man was arrested by military guards. Local people speculated that he had been arrested on the charges of espionage. However, despite the public interest in this arrest, the paper reported there was no such evidence that he was a German spy.[9] People were quick to leap to suspecting espionage in the early years of the war. Between the outbreak of hostilities and the end of 1914 spy fever and fear of German espionage reached its peak. David French noted that during the winter of 1914-15 the public became 'hysterical about the spy danger'.[10] Whilst this atmosphere of fear had reached its peak

---

[7]'Spy Scare at Braintree', *Essex Newsman*, 8 August 1914, p2

[8]Emden and Humphries, *All Quiet on the Home Front*, p68

[9]'The Spy Mania', *Yarmouth Independent*, 12 September 1914, p3

[10]David French, *Spy Fever*, p364-365

by the end of 1914 it had in no way reached its conclusion.

From 1915 onwards, fear of spies reduced but persisted in the east of England. In 1915 William Le Queux, who had stirred the public into a spy fever in the years preceding the war, released his latest work, *German Spies in England: An Exposure*. This detailed the methods and network of German intelligence agents in England, insinuating that this system had been covered up by the British government. The book sold more than 40,000 copies in one week alone, demonstrating the ongoing fascination the public still had with foreign spies operating in England.[11] It was believed that Zeppelin raids were guided by spies and fifth columnists. An article in the *Chelmsford Chronicle* stated how witnesses had claimed Zeppelin airships were being guided to their targets by German spies using their car headlights.[12] A further article in the *Chelmsford Chronicle* reported that spies along the east coast may be guiding Zeppelins. It also reported that people had mistaken shooting stars in the night sky for rockets they believed had been shot up by German spies to guide Zeppelins. Volunteer forces were regularly patrolling the coast looking for such guides.[13] Mistaking shooting stars for rockets shows how suspicion had clouded judgment. This, like the many other cases of spy fever, had serious repercussions. Thomas Farrow, a commercial traveller, was arrested in Essex in September 1916 for possessing illegal car

---

[11] Emden and Humphries, *All Quiet on the Home Front*, p66

[12] 'The Spies Defeated and Captured', *Chelmsford Chronicle*, 24 November 1916, p4

[13] 'The Night Patrol', *Chelmsford Chronicle*, 13 October 1916, p5

headlights. This would, in ordinary circumstances, have been considered a minor and trivial offence. In the madness that plagued the country in the early years of the First World War, it was claimed by many that he was using these headlights to aid Zeppelins and was thus suspected of espionage.[14]

The MP for the Norfolk constituency of Kings Lynn, Holcombe Ingleby, publicly expressed his belief that spies were aiding Zeppelins along the east coast by using car headlights.[15] Holcombe's remarks – and by others in the nation's political establishment – legitimised public fears.

By 1916 the extent of the spy fever significantly decreased from the levels of the first two years of the war. In 1916, for example, there were only 17 articles in local newspapers regarding the topic of espionage, some 51 by the end of 1917 and, finally, only 34 by the end of the war in 1918. One reason for the drop-off in concern may have been the increased difficulties facing German spies attempting to operate spy networks by the later stages of the war.[16] German espionage failures (allied to Security Services successes) meant that the ubiquitous German spy was no longer a feature of newspaper headlines. Public attention was turning towards the sheer magnitude and brutality of the fighting in the war. There grew a greater recognition that Britain and Germany

---

[14]Porter, *Clacton on Sea*, p44

[15]Browning, *Norfolk Coast*, p55

[16]BNA <https://www.britishnewspaperarchive.co.uk/search/results> [accessed 14 April 2019]

were locked in a total war, the world's first industrialised war.

Fear of German spies and espionage was rife in the east of England in the First World War. It resulted from a number of factors. Chief amongst them was the British government's increasingly poor relations with an emergent Germany in the decades preceding the war. As rivalry deepened, the two countries engaged in a kind of cold war with Britain and Germany engaged in competition on all fronts – military, economic, industrial, and diplomatic. This growing sense of competition is most clearly shown over the naval arms race. But there were other issues, such as German demands for a more equal share of colonies.

There was a genuine belief in the government and the public, that Germany posed a substantial threat to Britain, with espionage playing a key role in the undeclared war. This hostility, both within the government and public, inspired the genre of spy literature. This brought fears of Germany to a mass audience. There was a widespread public belief that they were surrounded in every street, town, and occupation by German spies. As a result of these decades of tension, when war with Germany finally broke out, the public were thrown into a state of frenzy and fear towards anyone even slightly suspicious, and especially towards people of German heritage. The outbreak of war with Germany confirmed that these prejudices were in fact, correct. Local newspapers of the east of England pandered to a major public fascination with the threat of espionage. The number of articles would have been a constant reminder of the threat faced. At the same time, local newspapers also shed light on the various ways in which fellow members of the public were affected, often in abhorrent ways. People were subject to extreme suspicion and false, baseless accusations of espionage by the clearly frightened and paranoid neighbours.

Spies of the Kaiser: Plotting the Downfall of England, William Le Queux, 1915.

Luton Times and Advertiser, 11 September 1914. Articles such as this enforced in the minds of the community that German spies were embedded within the local population and were an overarching threat to their daily lives.

CIVILIANS AS SPIES.

These precautionary outbursts, however, are perhaps not altogether unjustified, for Gurkhas are unpleasant enemies on dark nights, and in many places the trenches of the Indians and the Germans are only a few yards apart.

In this quarter a bombardment of the German trenches was carried out during the day, but the effect is not known. In the centre one of our battalions took an opportunity of opening fire on a German working party, and caused considerable loss.

Evidence of spying on the part of civilians was obtained on this day. A man in plain clothes was observed in the hostile trenches pointing out our positions. A German aviator dropped six bombs on Hazebrouck with little effect.

Since it has been so frequently stated that our howitzers have obtained "direct hits" on the enemy's gun emplacements, perhaps it is as well to explain what this means in terms of damage done to the enemy. In the most unfavourable case to us it means that one of our shells, charged with many pounds of lyddite, and fitted with a percussion fuse, has detonated on the parapet of an emplacement. The result would be that a number of the detachment might be killed or wounded, but that the gun would probably not be seriously damaged. In the most favourable case it would mean that the shell has detonated in the emplacement itself or actually on the gun or its mounting. This would almost certainly imply the destruction of both gun and detachment.

Halesworth Times and East Suffolk Advertiser, 22 December 1914.

7

PARANOIA VERSUS REALITY

Were the Reactions of the Public and Government Rational in their Fear of German Espionage and Invasion Efforts?

HOW DID THE FEARS OF AN invasion compare to the reality of German military plans? Were fears of invasion and espionage rational and justifiable?

Tensions between the two powers gathered pace with the succession of Kaiser Wilhelm II as Emperor in 1888. He soon abandoned the policy of international restraint favoured by the long-time German Chancellor Otto von Bismarck. The new Kaiser favoured a more aggressive foreign policy in order to assert Germany's position as the leading power in Europe. This more combative stance by Germany can be seen by its involvement in colonial disputes and its decision to substantially increase the size of its Imperial Navy. This was seen in Britain as direct challenge to the Royal Navy and its control of the seas.

As a result of the shift in policy initiated by the Kaiser, German military planners began to draw up plans for a possible invasion of Britain from 1895 onwards. Admiral

Eduard von Knorr, the Commander of the German Imperial Navy, was one of the leading architects of the invasion plans. In 1897 he presented his findings to the Kaiser. Von Knorr's plans outlined a scenario in which, following a declaration of war between the two nations, Germany, provided it acted swiftly, could launch a pre-emptive strike against the Royal Navy, followed by an immediate landing of troops before the British fleet spread across the globe could be mobilized.[1]

These invasion plans gained more credibility as the year went on. By November a more detailed plan by the German Naval Staff was presented to von Knorr: 'Project Memorandum: An Operation Against Antwerp'. The plan concluded that to achieve a successful invasion of Britain, Germany would first need to gain access to further ports along the North Sea by occupying the low countries of Belgium and the Netherlands. Ports there offered one of the quickest routes to Britain. This plan differed from the earlier proposals by von Knorr as it would require these actions to be taken 24 hours *before* a formal declaration of war.[2]

The German Navy's plan for an invasion of Great Britain was not supported by all of the German military establishment. Alfred von Schlieffen, for example, the Chief of the German General Staff, believed invasion to be highly impractical. However, he did recognise the benefit to military

---

[1] H.R. Moon, 'The Invasion of the United Kingdom: Public Controversy and Official Planning, 1888-1918', PhD Thesis, Kings College London, OCLC 53593359, July 1968, pp653-657

[2] J. Steinberg, 'A German Plan for the Invasion of Holland and Belgium, 1897' in P.M. Kennedy, *The War Plans of the Great Powers: 1880-1914* (Abingdon, Oxon Routledge, 1979), pp155-156

occupation of the Low Countries in the event of a two-front war with France and Russia. As a result, von Schlieffen supported plans for an invasion, and the views of the Naval Staff. They believed an invasion should be swift and must force a quick surrender before the Royal Navy could cut off German supply lines.[3] However, the newly appointed State Secretary of the German Imperial Naval Office opposed the plan. He believed no invasion of the United Kingdom could even be contemplated until the German Navy matched the Royal Navy in its size and strength.[4]

Despite the flurry of disagreements, however, planning continued during 1898 and more detailed proposals were put forward. The German Navy, after much consideration, believed that without prior preparation it would take at least eight days before any amphibious landing could take place, which would give the Royal Navy more time to mobilise their ships and less time for the German Army to achieve its objectives in Britain before the supply lines could be threatened. There were also disagreements on the size of the army needed to invade the United Kingdom, with the Navy suggesting that only three army corps would be necessary, whereas the army believed no fewer than eight would be needed. This more or less confirms von Schlieffen's belief that every available soldier would be needed to carry out the plan. However, whilst logistics and feasibility of the operation were hotly debated in military circles, views of potential landing sites for the invading German troops were

---

[3]H.R. Moon, pp658-660

[4]H.R. Moon, p662

unanimous. The chiefs of the navy and army agreed that landings along the south coast or along the river Thames would be near impossible due to the heavy concentration of coastal and inland defences. Landings north of the River Humber due to its distance from the capital were also ruled out. Planners from the army preferred a target as close as possible to London. As a result of these assessments and further reconnaissance work, military planners settled on three potential landing areas in the event of an invasion: south of the River Humber in north Lincolnshire close to the militarily vital port of Grimsby; the East Anglian coast from the Norfolk town of Great Yarmouth to the Suffolk town of Southwold; and finally, the Suffolk coast from Southwold to Orford Ness.[5] Von Schlieffen and other military planners deemed the coast between Great Yarmouth and Aldeburgh to be the ideal landing site due to its proximity to London, as well as major ports vital to an invasion's success such as Harwich and Felixstowe.

German military planning put the east of England directly in the landing zone, the first stage of a drive towards London. The east of England would bear the full brunt of a German military invasion. This view was shared by British home defence planners. Despite these advanced plans, any intention to invade Britain was shelved in January 1899 due to the difficulties that would be involved in any invasion attempt. First, von Knorr believed that any invasion attempt would be futile without military allies and, in this case, Germany's two main allies, Austria-Hungary and Italy, were too weak

---

[5] H.R. Moon, pp665-669

militarily to be capable of any real support. Secondly, and perhaps most importantly, both the naval and army staffs agreed that the assembly of any invasion force without alerting Britain, or her allies would be impossible. Britain would have time to mobilize the Royal Navy into an effective defence. This theory was vindicated by the inability of the German military to maintain secrecy during its invasion of Kia Chow during the Boxer Rebellion in August 1897. Thirdly, in the Anglo-German naval arms race, Germany was currently the losing party and far from any sort of parity with the Royal Navy. German involvement in the Far East, meant that Germany's naval resources were being seriously stretched. Finally, army chiefs such as von Schlieffen believed that, due to the European system of alliances, any European conflict would likely draw in both France and Russia. This would leave German troops dangerously overstretched on three fronts and unable to properly defend the German borders from French attacks in the west and Russian attacks in the east. Despite this, however, some within the German military staff did still believe invasion was possible. Lieutenant General Colmar Freiherr von der Goltz, Commander of the Prussian Engineer Corps, saw the reduced British home defence forces, due to the ongoing Second Boer War in the early years of the 20th century, as being an ideal opportunity to attempt an invasion. This, however, was rejected by the German military staff.

From that point on, under the leadership of Admiral von Tirpitz, the growth in the size and capabilities of the German fleet was not to be used to challenge the supremacy of the Royal Navy, nor was it be used to make invasion a possibility;

rather its main purpose was to make the United Kingdom more amenable to provide concessions to Germany.

Upon the outbreak of the conflict, plans to invade Britain were not revised, as German intelligence overestimated the strength of British coastal defences and, as we have seen, naval objectives were instead targeted at smaller raids of coastal towns, aimed to force smaller pockets of the Royal Navy to intervene where the German fleet might have the advantage. The reality of the military situation was that Germany simply never had the capability to invade the United Kingdom. Whilst it is true Germany controlled many ports in Belgium, which could be used to launch an invasion of the east coast, it had no access to the other vital ports situated in the Netherlands which would have provided greater naval capacity, as well as a closer direct proximity to the desired landing beaches of East Anglia. The German Navy did not manage to match the size of the Royal Navy and never reached a point where it could act freely on a large scale in the North Sea, instead confining itself to smaller raids and unrestricted submarine warfare.

Germany simply never had the manpower to even attempt an invasion of Britain during the Great War. Germany failed to successfully carry out the von Schlieffen plan. Central to the plan was the idea that the German Army would encircle Paris through Belgium and Northern France, forcing a swift surrender in the west, before turning the full might of their army east and onto Russia before her enormous army could fully mobilise. Instead, by the winter of 1914, Germany found itself in the position German High Command feared the most – a two-front war. On the western front German troops were in the midst of a seemingly never-ending stalemate with French, British, and Belgian forces. In the east, the German army was deep into Russian territory whilst also simultaneously propping up the weak Austro-Hungarian army in their fight against Russia and, finally, the preservation of the German colonies abroad also required the presence of German troops. This position left German forces spread out over a vast area of Europe and the rest of the world, requiring millions of soldiers to simply hold these fronts, fought for with an intensity and brutality unimaginable hitherto.

****

In the 1890s it seems rational that the government, military authorities, as well as the public, would fear an invasion of the counties in the east of England. Germany planned for an invasion of Britain in the event of war. It is not clear that the British government were directly aware of German military plans and thus could not be certain if Germany was considering invasion.

German military planning cannot be used to entirely rationalise public fears of invasion in the east of England. The public would have no insight into British intelligence, nor could they possibly know of German military planning. Whilst this is certainly true, there are also many factors that convinced the civil and military authorities, as well as the general public that Germany was preparing for an invasion of the British Isles. For example, towards the end of the 19th century, Britain found itself being challenged in its position as the most powerful industrialised nation in Europe. Germany was far more populated, it became economically more powerful, and more industrialised, following unification in 1871. Germany, under the direction of the young Kaiser Wilhelm II, became more militaristic and aggressive in its foreign policy. Germany rapidly built a navy to challenge the British fleet. Germany posed a significant challenge to Britain's colonial interests. Even though Britain did not have conclusive proof that Germany was actively planning invasion, these factors could rationally lead to the assumption that Germany was preparing for war with Britain. Logically therefore, an invasion might be attempted.

In the early 20th century British military intelligence concluded that Germany was planning invasion based on a series of amphibious landing exercises by both the German army and navy in 1901. Perhaps this appears, with the benefit of hindsight, to be an overreaction.

Given the ever-growing tensions between the two nations before the war and Germany's increasingly belligerent foreign policy, when war broke out in August 1914 all fears of invasion must have been felt as justified by the British. The invasion of Belgium and northern France and the barrage of propaganda that came with these events would have led any reasonable person to believe Britain could be next in line. It is, of course, important to emphasise that early in the war when invasion fears in the east of England were at their peak, that it was far from clear that the war was going to culminate in victory for the Allies.

In the early years of the war Germany threatened many times to break the stalemate on the western front, knocking

France out of the war and leaving the British Isles ripe for invasion. The collapse of the Russian Empire in 1917 and Russian withdrawal from the war, meant Germany was free to deploy its entire military resources onto the western front. Even in the last stages of the war, Germany had hopes that they could win – hopes that were only dashed with the failure of the German Spring Offensive. But that offensive *did* threaten to overwhelm the British and French forces. It very nearly succeeded in breaking the years of attrition and stalemate.

Despite Germany never reaching a stage where it could with confidence attempt an invasion of Britain, for the British observer at the time it was not irrational to believe that invasion could be attempted. There was a distinct possibility that the war on the continent could turn against the British and French forces. Invasion plans drafted by the German high command proved the reality and rationality behind these fears. Both the British and the Germans believed that East Anglia would be the target of an invading force. Norfolk and Suffolk coasts were the favoured landing beaches for any proposed German offensive. Naturally this meant that the east of England would have borne the brunt of the invasion onslaught. Local fears were, therefore, entirely rational. The threat of invasion was not a ludicrous fantasy. German naval raids against towns on the East Anglian coast, as well as the frequent Zeppelin raids, could be interpreted as German loosening-up manoeuvres, and a prelude to invasion. It helps to make some of the seemingly irrational actions of the public much more understandable.

Concerns about invasion, fears of espionage, and German

agents operating in the east of England, can be seen in retrospect to be more based on reality and rationality than we now give credit. Invasion was never truly a working option for the German military and was only a possibility. By contrast espionage was an ever-present legitimate threat both before and during the war. In the decades preceding the war, German spy rings were operating in Britain. However, these spy rings were ludicrously small by modern standards and were mostly restricted to the German navy intelligence which was small and poorly funded. The small scale of the German spy rings can be seen from the actions of the Secret Service (the precursor to MI5). Between August 1911 and July 1914, the Secret Service arrested only ten suspects, a tiny number when compared to the widespread fear that existed in Britain at this time.[6] Whilst this figure is small, it is worth bearing in mind that British counterespionage was a new concept and was in the process of rapid development. This may have limited German capabilities. By the outbreak of war, German spy rings had not sufficiently developed from their pre-war strength and organisation, and continued to have only a miniscule presence in Britain. The German naval intelligence officer responsible for pre-war and wartime German intelligence in Britain, Gustav Steinhauer, struggled to gain success with his spy ring in Britain. Much of the intelligence from his spies was militarily useless to the German war effort. An example is the spy Carl Hans Lody's untrue report that Russian troops had been seen marching towards the south

---

[6]<http://www.nationalarchives.gov.uk/pathways/firstworldwar/spotlights/espionage.htm> [accessed 13 June 2020]

of England from Aberdeen.[7] The methods of the British counter-espionage system developed so quickly and effectively that the few German spies remaining in Britain struggled to communicate effectively with their superiors in Berlin. In all, the small scale of the German espionage efforts in Britain can be seen by the fact that between August 1914 and September 1917, only 31 German spies were arrested. Estimates suggest that no more than 120 Germans operated in Britain during the four years of the war.[8][9]

That there was a German spy ring operating in Britain gave some reality to the pre-war spy fever that existed at all levels of society. This intense spy fever could be seen as an irrational overreaction. The widespread pre-war belief that Britain, and especially the east of England, was teeming with German spies disguised as waiters, teachers, and neighbours, was completely overblown and irrational compared to the actual German spy network. However, as with invasion fears, we are looking at people's reactions with the obvious benefit of hindsight. The deep-seated fear of German spies before the war can be seen to be more rational when we think about the rising temperature of tensions between Britain and Germany. In the early 20th century, the fulcrum of Anglo-German mistrust was the naval arms race between the two countries. Considering the geo-political facts of the era, it would make complete sense for Germany to have an effective intelligence network in Britain, to monitor political and

---

[7]Ibid

[8]Ibid

[9]https://www.h-net.org/reviews/showpdf.php?id=12283

popular opinion in the country, to observe the Royal Navy and the state of British military preparedness.

Regardless of the realities of the situation, the sheer number of books published at this time detailing the threat of German spies, coupled with the fact that this view was shared by the British press and many in the government, would convince many members of the public that their fears were not unreasonable. The same can be said of the British civil and military authorities. They could not, due to the nature of espionage, have conclusively known that larger and more effective German spy rings were not operational in the country. However, it could be argued they should have been less sensationalist in the expression of their fears.

The true extent of the German spy danger was not known. It would be natural to assume there would be vast amounts of spying by both Germany and Britain. The rationality of the ways in which the authorities and the public of the counties of eastern England reacted to these fears, is up for debate. In respect of government and military authorities, many of the counter-espionage measures were perfectly rational, given that Britain was a nation at war. The Defence of the Realm Act (DORA) of 1914, for all its flaws, was a rational piece of legislation. It was necessary for the authorities to have wartime powers and to accept that normal peacetime civil liberties would be curbed, to minimise the threat posed by espionage. Furthermore, the expansion of the intelligence services is a reasonable war time measure and especially so given their small scale and limited powers before the outbreak of war.

The treatment of those of German ancestry or citizenship

is far less defensible. The restrictions placed on these people, via the Aliens Restriction Act, was clearly rooted in a general xenophobia – or to be more specific – Germanophobia. There were far too many harsh restrictions on those of German heritage. Restrictions such as the forced curfew, registration of address, as well as expulsion from the east coast, were unjustified and unfair in comparison to the restrictions imposed upon the rest of the British public. Imprisonment of all German citizens and those of German background living in Britain was wholly unjust especially in light of the small scale of the German spy networks. It could be argued that this was a safer option for these people than being exposed to intense anti-German animosity. I do not believe this formed the main motivation for the government's decision for mass incarceration. From the government's perspective, Britain was engaged in a 'fight to the finish' war with Germany. It should have had concerns about the potential threat posed by the 50,000 Germans living and working in the country. Whilst expulsion from the east coast seems unjust, we must remember that the east coast was the most likely landing spot for the invading German army. It was a particularly sensitive area for the British army and navy. Arguably there were more moderate ways of minimising a potential threat from the British-German population.

On the whole, public attitudes to rumours of threat of German spying in the counties of the east of England were reasonable considering the military importance of that area. What was not rational was the often hysterical way they treated suspicious persons including those of German heritage. They were often victimised by the public, who believed spies were everywhere. This was the result of decades of Anglo-German hostility, the immense popularity of spy literature, press propaganda combined with government warnings to be vigilant of German spies. It is unsurprising that the public reacted as it did.

The balance of rationality and the climate of fear created by war is difficult to strike. Whilst in the modern day we can see with hindsight the reality behind these fears, we have to carefully consider the information available then as well as the prevailing ethos of that time.

Kaiser Wilhelm II was Emperor of Germany between 15 June 1888 and 9 November 1918 and was one of the key figures in the build up to the First World War. Upon his ascension to the throne he ditched the policy of international restraint and cooperation favoured by the long-time chancellor Otto von Bismarck, instead adopting a more aggressive foreign policy including the rapid expansion of the German Navy to challenge the Royal Navy and a more confrontationalist colonial policy.

Ernst Wilhelm Eduard von Knorr was a German admiral in the pre-war years and was the first to propose military plans to invade the United Kingdom to the Kaiser. His plans recognised the inferiority of the German Navy to the Royal Navy and thus suggested that any invasion would require a pre-emptive strike on the Royal Navy followed by an immediate invasion before the fleet could fully mobilise and group.

Field Marshall Alfred von Schlieffen was Chief of the German Imperial Staff from 1891-1906 and is most famous for the von Schlieffen plan which aimed to swiftly invade France through Belgium, encircling Paris and the bulk of the French army, thus forcing a swift surrender.

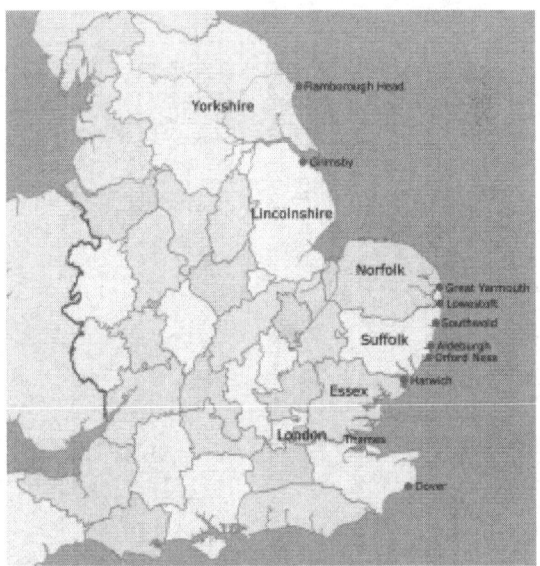

Map depicting favoured German landing sites in the event of an invasion of Britain.

Carl Hans Lody was a German spy active in Britain in the first few months of the war. He was first approached by the German Naval intelligence in the months preceding the war, and in late August 1914, following the outbreak of war, was sent to Britain posing as American citizen Charles A. Ingles, where he went to Scotland to observe the activities of the Royal Navy. Fearing for his own safety following the increasingly hostile treatment many Germans faced, Lody fled to Ireland but was eventually captured, tried and executed.

CONCLUSION

Reflections on Public and Government Responses to the Fears of German Invasion and Espionage in the East of England during the First World War

DISRAELI ON THE FORMATION OF THE German Empire:

> ... Let me impress upon the attention of the House the character of this war between France and Germany. It is no common war, like the war between Prussia and Austria, or like the Italian war in which France was engaged some years ago; nor is it like the Crimean War.
>
> This war represents the German revolution, a greater political event than the French revolution of last century. I don't say a greater, or as great a social event. What its social consequences may be are in the future. Not a single principle in the management of our foreign affairs, accepted by all statesmen for guidance up to six months ago, any longer exists. There is not a diplomatic tradition which has not been swept away. You have a new world, new influences at work, new and unknown objects and dangers with which to cope, at present involved in that obscurity incident to novelty in such affairs. We used to have discussions in this House about the balance of power. Lord Palmerston, eminently a practical man, trimmed the ship of State and shaped its policy with a view to preserve an equilibrium in Europe. [...] But what has really come to pass? The balance of power has been entirely

destroyed, and the country which suffers most, and feels the effects of this great change most, is England.

This was the start of the British story that led to the Great War. Disraeli's acute observations stated the problem facing British diplomacy. Instead of certainty of policy there was changeability. Relations with France were ambiguous and from time to time, hostile. There was one fact: that of German supremacy in mainland Europe. 'Where next?' was a vexing political and diplomatic problem for Britain from that point onwards.

From the Franco-Prussian war of 1870 after which the German Empire was created, rivalry between Britain and Germany grew. This rivalry was economic, political and colonial. From Britain's perspective increasing German militarism was combined with an aggressive German foreign policy – especially after Kaiser Wilhelm II's accession. This only reinforced the notion that dealing with the German threat was critical. Confrontation or competition seemed to be the only response. This policy response culminated in both the Anglo-French Entente and the naval arms race with Germany in the early 20th century.

Anxiety about German intentions was amplified in popular literature and the press. This anxiety was shared at all levels of society. The threat of a German invasion seemed real and

Source: Hansard, *Parliamentary Debates*, Ser. III, vol. cciv, February-March 1871, speech of 9 February 1871, pp81-82

Original English text reprinted in William Flavelle Moneypenny and George Earle Buckle, *The Life of Benjamin Disraeli, Earl of Beaconsfield*, new rev. ed. in 2 vols., vol. 2, *1860-1881* (London: John Murray, 1929), pp473-74

was feared. Britain's history of invasions lent credibility to the idea that there were numerous spies, saboteurs, and fifth columnists that accompany invasions. This influenced governmental as well as military policy and strategy. It had a special impact on the people living in eastern England. In the build up to the Great War these fears reached new levels of intensity.

In eastern England, paranoia and fear reached a climax in the first year of the war to mid-1915, but remained substantial for the most of the war's duration. The probability of invasion was viewed according to the apparent opportunity Germany would have had to conduct a landing. Some saw the stalemate on the western front as an opportunity for Germany to conduct a full-scale landing. Others saw the stalemate as disadvantage.

There is little doubt that contemporary opinion could change at any moment. Fear of invasion remained at high levels and was significant throughout 1914 to 1916. Thereafter, for the most part, it began to decline. Alarms developed spasmodically during the remaining years of the war driven by events and ever-changing perspectives of the civil and military authorities, and especially amongst those living in the counties of the east of England.

The war had the effect on the British people, but especially those living in the east of England, of losing civil liberties. This included losing the right to a civil trial, restrictions on movement, victimisation of minorities (notably people of German heritage) and the sequestration of private property. This was seen as justifiable in the context of a brutal enemy intent upon domination. The comprehensive nature of home defence planning meant more and more interventions from the state that affected individuals, which was new to Britain.

Events on the national scale affect the lives of ordinary people. This study shows just how profound the impact can be. It sheds light on the psychology of civilian warfare and the day-to-day effects war has on a nation. It is an aspect of the Great War which is little studied, and is consequently little appreciated.

BIBLIOGRAPHY

Primary Sources

1. Unpublished Manuscripts

(a) Official records

'DORA 1914, Chapter 29', in Legislation.Gov.UK

<http://www.legislation.gov.uk/ukpga/Geo5/4-5/29/contents/enacted> [accessed 1 April 2019]

'Guidance to the Civil Population of East Suffolk in the Event of a Landing by the Enemy on the Coast' in *St Edmundsbury Local History*

<http://www.stedmundsburychronicle.co.uk/galleryww1/galleryww1page_09.htm

'Internment of Enemy Aliens', R. McKenna, 7 December 1914, PRO, Cab. 37/122/182

'Memorandum on the principles governing the defence of the United Kingdom', 4 October 1910, PRO, Cab. 38/16/20

'Minutes of the meeting 18 December 1903', PRO, Cab. 38/3/84

'Minutes of the 125th meeting of the CID', 3 March 1914, PRO, Cab. 2/3, 4 & 5 Geo. 5, c. 12

'Minutes of the 129th meeting of the CID', 7 October 1914, PRO, Cab. 38/28/47

'Minutes of the 3rd meeting of the Sub-Committee', 12 July 1909, PRO, Cab. 16/8

PRO, Cab. 17/90, CID paper 181B, appendix v, July 1913

'Report and Proceedings', 22 October 1908, PRO, Cab. 16/3A

'Report and Proceedings of a sub-Committee of Imperial Defence, Appointed by the Prime Minister to Reconsider the Question of Oversea Attack', 22 October 1908, PRO, Cab. 16/3A

'Report by Major Anderson', 28 June 1919, PRO, DEFE 1/30, p104

'Report of a sub-committee', 24 July 1909, PRO, Cab. 16/8

'Report of a sub-committee', CID paper 47-A

2. Contemporary published sources

(a) Official publications

HC Parliamentary Debate, 26 July 1915, 73, col. 1930-8

Annuaire statistique de la Belgique et du Congo Belge, 1915-1919, Bruxelles, 1922, p100

(b) Newspapers and contemporary publications

'An Alien's Motor Car', *Essex Newsman*, 29 August 1914, p2

'A Costly Fire', *Essex Newsman*, 30 October 1915, p3

'Another Air Raid at Southend', *Essex Newsman*, 29 May 1915, p3

'1000 Appeals', *Essex Newsman*, 15 April 2015, p4

'Police Courts', *Essex Newsman*, 22 January 1916, p3

'Alien Fined for Harbouring His Wife', *Chelmsford Chronicle*, 28 August 1914, p2

'As to National Service', 20 August 1910, *The Lowestoft Journal*, p4

James Blyth, *The Swoop of the Vulture* (London: Digby, Long and Company, 1909)

BNA <https://www.britishnewspaperarchive.co.uk/search/results> [accessed 12 April 2019]

BNA <https://www.britishnewspaperarchive.co.uk/search/results> [accessed 14 April 2019]

BNA <https://www.britishnewspaperarchive.co.uk/search/results> [accessed 23 April 2019]

'Burston Recruitment Meeting', *Diss Express*, 26 February 1916, p4

Cambridge Independent Press, 30 April 1915, p6

'Chelmsford Minister and the Kaiser', *Essex Newsman*, 26 September 1914, p2

George Chesney, *The Battle of Dorking: Reminiscences of a Volunteer* (Oxford: Oxford City Press, 2010)

'Child Pinned with a Sword', *Suffolk and Essex Free Press*, 9 December 1914, p7

Chronicle, 6 November 1914, p5

'Danger of Invasion', *Chelmsford Chronicle*, 23 June 1916, p5

'Defence of the Realm Act', *Framlingham Weekly News*, 17 July 1915, p1

'Defence of the Realm – An Arrest at Chelmsford', *Essex Newsman*, 14 November 1914, p3

'East Suffolk County Council', *Diss Express*, 19 November 1915, p5

Essex County Standard, 7 November 1914, p8

Essex County Standard, 22 August 1914, p4

'Essex Volunteer Force', *Chelmsford Chronicle*, 13 October 1916, p5

'German Barbarities', *Cambridge Independent Press*, 11 September 1914, p6

'German Fined £100', *Chelmsford Chronicle*, 28 August 1914, p2

'German Spy Danger', *Suffolk and Essex Free Press*, 9 September 1914, p6

'How History Repeats Itself', *Chelmsford Chronicle*, 25 September 1914, p2

'In Case of a Raid', *Essex Newsman*, 5 December 1914, p1

'In Case of Invasion', *Bedfordshire Times and Independent*, 12 March 1915, p5

'In Case of Invasion', *Chelmsford Chronicle*, 25 December 1914, p4

'Letter to the Editor', *Cambridge Independent Press*, 25 September 1914, p4

'Maningtree Man Charged', *Chelmsford Chronicle*, 13 November 1914, p2

'Spy Scare at Braintree', *Essex Newsman*, 8 August 1914, p2

'Sunk by Mine', *Diss Express*, 11 September 1914

'The Annual Register', *The Times*, 10, 11 and 13 May 1915, p103

'The Night Patrol', *Chelmsford Chronicles*, 13 October 1916, p5

'The Spies Defeated and Captured', *Chelmsford Chronicle*, 24 November 1916, p4

'The Spy Mania', *Yarmouth Independent*, 12 September 1914, p3

The Times, 17 August 1914, p9

William Le Queux, *The Invasion of 1910* (London, 1906)

'Volunteer Training Corps', 23 July 1915, in *Diss Express*, p5

(c) Other contemporary published sources

'Borough of Dover Emergency Committee Poster on Evacuation Plans', in E.A. Pratt, *British Railways and the Great War* (London, Selwyn and Blout, 1921)

'City of Norwich Instructions for the Guidance of the Civil Population in the Event of a Landing by the Enemy in this County' in E.A. Pratt, *British Railways and the Great War* (London, Selwyn and Blout, 1921)

'DORA poster on Naval and Military powers, issued 1914', in *National Archives* <http://www.nationalarchives.gov.uk/education/britain1906to1918/g5/cs1/g5cs1s2c.htm> [accessed 1 April 2019]

'Dunmow District Emergency Instructions', in *Essex Voices Past* <http://www.essexvoicespast.com/war-and-remembrance-dunmows-emergency-committee/> [accessed 20 March 2019]

'Historical Sketch', 1921, PRO, WO, 32/10776, p12

'Historical Sketch', 1921, PRO, WO, 32/10776, p20

Kell Papers (Frost), lecture by Vernon Kell headed 'Scottish Chief Constables', 26 February 1925, p24

Kell Papers (Frost), lecture on 'Security Intelligence work' by Holt Wilson, June 1939, p11

Minutes of the Latchingford Parish Council, 10 December 1914, in Catriona Pennell, '"The Germans Have Landed!". Invasion Fears in the South-East of England, August to December 1914', p109

'Poster on DORA Regulations, issued 1914' in *National Archives* <http://www.nationalarchives.gov.uk/education/britain1906to1918/g5/cs1/g5cs1s2b.htm> [accessed 1 April 2019]

3. Memoirs and autobiographies

Arnold Bennett writing on 10 August 1914, in Catriona Pennell, '"The Germans Have Landed!": Invasion Fears in the South-East of England, August to December 1914', p102

Joe Cook, 'August 1914', in Catriona Pennell, '"The Germans Have Landed!": Invasion Fears in the South-East of England, August to December 1914', p105

The Imperial War Museum Sound Archives, 7375: Reel 1

4. Articles published online

<http://www.essexrecordofficeblog.co.uk/zeppelins-over-essex/.> [accessed 27 June 2020]

Transcript of Rose Luard's letter describing the landing of Zeppelin L31 in Little Wigborough, 24 September 1916 (D/DLu 76)

Secondary sources

1. Books, articles and essays

Ian F. Beckett and Keith Simpson, *A Nation in Arms: The British Army in the First World War* (Pen and Sword Military)

Stephen Browning, *Norfolk Coast in the Great War: King's Lynn, Hunstanton, Sherringham, Cromer and Great Yarmouth* (Barnsley: Pen and Sword Military, 2017)

Stephen Constantine, M.W. Kirby, M.B. Rose eds., *The First World War in British History* (London: Edward Arnold, 1995)

Gerard J. DeGroot, *Blighty: British Society in the Era of the Great War* (London: Adison Wesley Longman Limited, 1996)

K.D. Ewing and C.A. Gearty eds., *The Struggle for Civil Liberties: Political Freedoms and the Rule of Law in Britain, 1914-1945* (Oxford: Oxford University Press, 2000)

David French, 'Spy Fever in Britain, 1900-1915', *The Historical Journal*, Vol 21, No 2 (June, 1978)

Nicoletta Gullace, *The Blood of Our Sons: Men, Women and the Renegotiation of British Citizenship During the Great War* (Palgrave Macmillan, 2002)

Cate Haste, *Keep the Home Fires Burning* (London: Penguin Books, 1977)

Nicholas Hiley, 'Counter Espionage and Security in Great Britain during the First World War', *The English History Review*, Vol 101, No 400 (July, 1986)

Richard Van Emden and Steve Humphries, *All Quiet on the Home Front: An Oral History of Life in Britain During the First World War* (London: Headline Book Publishing, 2003)

Paul Kennedy, *The Rise of the Anglo-German Antagonism 1860-1914* (London: Allen and Unwin, 1982)

D.H. Lawrence, *Selected Letters* (Harmondsworth, 1978)

D.H. Lawrence, *Kangaroo* (1923; reprint Harmondsworth, 1985)

Arthur Marwick, *The Deluge: British Society and the First World War* (Basingstoke: Macmillan Education, 1961)

H.R. Moon, 'The Invasion of the United Kingdom: Public Controversy and Official Planning, 1888-1918', PhD Thesis, King's College London, OCLC 53593359, July 1968

Troy Paddock ed., *World War I and Propaganda* (Boston: Brill, 2014)

Peter Padfield, *The Great Naval Race: The Anglo-German Naval Rivalry 1900-1914* (London: Hart-Davis, MacGibbon, 1974)

Panikos Panayi, *Prisoners of Britain: German Civilian and Combatant Internees During the First World War* (Manchester University Press, 2012)

Catriona Pennell, '"The Germans Have Landed!": Invasion Fears in the South-East of England, August to December 1914', History of Warfare, Vol 49, (2008)

Ken Porter, *Clacton-on-Sea and the Surrounding Coastline in the Great War* (Barnsley: Pen and Sword Books, 2017)

E.A. Pratt, *British Railways and the Great War* (London: Selwyn and Blout, 1921)

Matthew S. Seligmann, *Spies in Uniform: British Military and Naval Intelligence on the Eve of the First World War* (Oxford: Oxford University Press, 2006)

J. Steinberg, 'A German Plan for the Invasion of Holland and Belgium, 1897' in P.M. Kennedy, *The War Plans of the Great Powers: 1880-1914* (Abingdon: Oxon Routledge, 1979)

Graydon A. Tunstall, 'Austria-Hungary and the Brusilov Offensive of 1916', *The Historian*, 70 (1): 30-53 [p52]. doi:10.1111/j.1540-6563.2008.00202.x

Various authors, *Great Speeches of the War* (London: Hazell, Watson & Viney, 1915), p1

Robert Weldon Whalen, *Bitter Wounds: German Victims of the Great War, 1914-1939* (Ithaca, 1984)

J.M. Winter, *The Great War and the British People* (Basingstoke: Macmillan Education, 1985)

2. Unpublished secondary sources

H.R. Moon, 'The Invasion of the United Kingdom: Public Controversy and Official Planning, 1888-1918' (PhD Thesis, University of London, 1968)

3. Website articles

< https://www.edp24.co.uk/features/great-yarmouth-s-lucky-escape-and-the-failed-bombardment-1-3830399> [accessed 26 August 2020]

<http://www.nationalarchives.gov.uk/pathways/firstworldwar/spotlights/espionage.htm> [accessed 13 June 2020]

4. Book Reviews

Jeffrey Verhey reviewing Thomas Boghardt, *Spies of the Kaiser: German Covert Operations in Great Britain During the First World War Era* (Houndmills: Palgrave Macmillan, 2005) in https://www.h-net.org/reviews/showpdf.php?id=12283 [accessed 19 June 2020]